Quentin Tarantino

On Directors Series

John Ford
Alfred Hitchcock

Quentin
Tarantino

Edward Gallafent

PEARSON
Longman

Harlow, England • London • New York • Boston • San Francisco • Toronto
Sydney • Tokyo • Singapore • Hong Kong • Seoul • Taipei • New Delhi
Cape Town • Madrid • Mexico City • Amsterdam • Munich • Paris • Milan

Pearson Education Limited
Edinburgh Gate
Harlow
Essex CM20 2JE
England

and Associated Companies throughout the world

Visit us on the World Wide Web at:
www.pearsoned.co.uk

First published 2006

ISBN-13: 978-0-582-47304-1
ISBN-10: 0-582-47304-7

British Library Cataloguing-in-Publication Data
A catalogue record for this book is available from the British Library

Library of Congress Cataloging-in-Publication Data
Gallafent, Edward.
    Quentin Tarantino / Ed Gallafent.
        p. cm. — (On directors series)
    Includes bibliographical references and index.
    ISBN 0-582-47304-7
        1. Tarantino, Quentin—Criticism and interpretation.   I. Title.   II. Series.

    PN1998.3.T358G35 2006
    791.4302′33092—dc22

                                                    2005045611

10 9   8   7   6   5   4   3   2   1
10   09   08   07   06

Typeset in 10/13pt Giovanni Book by 35
Printed and bound in China
WC/01

The publisher's policy is to use paper manufactured from sustainable forests.

Contents

Acknowledgements

The original conception of this book was developed through extensive discussions with Alexander Ballinger. I thank him for his energy and good judgement, and his encouragement and advice in some of my anxious moments. I have also benefited from the enthusiasm of Gavin McLean, who has been both flexible and helpful in the later stages of the writing. Thanks also to Will Eaves, who must bear the responsibility of first causing me to write on Tarantino by inviting me to review the early wave of biographies for the *Times Literary Supplement* in 1995.

I am grateful to the University of Warwick for the grant of sabbatical leave during which this book was planned and commenced. My colleagues in the Film and Television Studies Department at Warwick have created as benign a context for writing and working as I know: a couple of them are mentioned in the following pages, but I should like to thank all of them. In addition, there are a few cineastes whose conversations with me about Tarantino have been invaluable, both cheering and intellectually stimulating: I particularly thank Peter Falconer, Ed Lamberti and James Zborowski.

Finally, I wish to thank my editor at Pearson, Mary Lince, and my copy editor, Ron Hawkins.

Over the last four years, many students working with me on Hollywood cinema have teased me with friendly enquiries as to the book's progress. I hope they enjoy it, and think it was worth the wait.

As Director

1992   *Reservoir Dogs* (Dog Eat Dog Productions/Live America Inc.)
1994   *Pulp Fiction* (A Band Apart/Jersey Films/Miramax Films)
1995   *Four Rooms* (Segment: 'The Man from Hollywood') (A Band Apart/Miramax Films)
1997   *Jackie Brown* (A Band Apart/Lawrence Bender Productions/Mighty Mighty Afrodite Productions/Miramax Films)
2003   *Kill Bill Vol.1* (Miramax Films/A Band Apart/Super Cool ManChu)
2004   *Kill Bill Vol.2* (Miramax Films/A Band Apart/Super Cool ManChu)

As Writer

True Romance (1993 film directed by Tony Scott, screenplay by Tarantino)

Natural Born Killers (1994 film directed by Oliver Stone, story by Tarantino)

From Dusk till Dawn (1996 film directed by Robert Rodriguez, screenplay by Tarantino)

Background

Life consists of the personal experiments of each of us, and the point of an experiment is that it shall succeed. What we contribute is our treatment of the material, our rendering of the text, our style.
(Henry James (1890), *The Tragic Muse*, Vol.I, Chapter IX)

The feature films directed by Quentin Tarantino between 1991 and 2004 have been variously admired for their styles, visual and verbal wit, ingeniousness of casting, narrative structure, choreography, their attitude to race and their treatment of violence. They have also been widely reviled, on the basis of most if not all of the same characteristics. Perhaps just as significantly they have also been treated with hauteur by critics willing to discuss (say) Paul Thomas Anderson or Todd Haynes or the Coen Brothers, as if a brief, or tacit, assertion that the films are clearly beneath notice might be the best way of dealing with them.

All of these discussions seem to point us towards two conclusions. One is that this interest, however expressed, has helped to make Tarantino one of the most widely known of the world's current film-makers. The other is that we are by no means agreed as to what to make of some of these effects and techniques on film. The object of this study is to ask some questions about Tarantino's work. Some of them are obvious, about violence or storytelling. Others are quite detailed and specific, and some examples of these are as follows.

How does Tarantino treat establishing shots? Why does he seem to prefer those which take the form of written announcements? Does he consciously avoid presenting the American crowd, or any image of men and women deliberately gathered together in the role of spectators? Why does he avoid the rhetoric of the speech of the dying, the rendition of words insured against insignificance by the imminent death of the character? How does he depict power, or villainy? How should we feel about the endings of his movies? Could he possibly be concealing that quality which so many sides

1

of American culture hate to acknowledge, a degree of melancholy? Nobody would (I believe) accuse Tarantino of being solemn. Is he serious? This book attempts to address these questions and others like them, and in some cases offers an answer to them.

Anyone writing on Tarantino in 2005 must have the sense that his or her conclusions are provisional. This is in part a matter of hindsight, an awareness that this is not an easily predictable career. It would hardly have been possible, after *Pulp Fiction*, to guess the nature of the next films. But it could be argued that what we have now is a body of work that is big enough to interrogate. There are so far five (I am already judging, by taking *Kill Bill* as two films) directed films, a few screenplays filmed by others, and some small to medium roles as an actor.

This study covers what I think most of those interested in contemporary Hollywood cinema (even his detractors) would take to be the defining work that Tarantino has produced: *Reservoir Dogs, Pulp Fiction, Jackie Brown, Kill Bill Vol.1* and *Vol.2*. In addition to this, I shall be looking at two screenplays, *True Romance* and *Natural Born Killers* (I regret that for reasons of space I shall not be covering *From Dusk till Dawn*).

The two elements that I see as contributing to the films could be broadly summed up under the headings of the traditional and the modern. Under traditional we could place the commonly quoted fact about Tarantino that he is a cinephile, with an enviably extensive and informed knowledge of a wide range of world cinema. Under the same heading I also argue that Tarantino is very much an American film-maker and writer, and that his work is informed by the concerns and preoccupations that have tradition-ally interested American artists. Under the heading of the modern I place Tarantino's enthusiastic fascination with the film technologies of the present time. Thus my argument can be sketched as saying that the energy of Tarantino's cinema derives from his having gone back to traditional American subjects and images and married them to the expressive possi-bilities that are properties of current cinema, increasingly available to him after the career-establishing first feature.

So far the action of Tarantino's films has been set insistently in the present. His flashbacks extend only to the earlier parts of the lives of his contemporary characters; where the remote past is invoked, such as Captain Koons' story of the watch's early history in *Pulp Fiction*, or Bill's anecdote about Pai Mei and the monk in *Kill Bill*, the camera remains with the teller of the tale. Thus pieties and images from the whole span of the past are experienced in the present, and a crucial part of their meaning is to do with the terms in which it is possible to use them, and those in which it is not possible. The assertion of meaning for those who inhabit worlds in which meanings are assumed to be irrelevant, or avoidable, or unavailable – it is this that ties *Reservoir Dogs* to *Kill Bill*, as I intend to show. This seems to me to be the point of distinction between Tarantino's work and the impulse of postmodernism: the contrast to what Perry Anderson beautifully describes as 'the peculiarly postmodern loss of any sense of the past, in a hidden contamination of the actual by the wistful' (*The Origins of Postmodernity*, p.59). The sense of the past is exactly what Tarantino's characters do not, or find they cannot, lose. The question is what they will do in the present with this fact of possession by the past.

In what follows I do not attempt to give a summarising reading of each film. The chapters concentrate on different aspects and elements of one or two (in one case, all three) of the first three films. The exception, simply because it was not released until most of the other chapters had been largely written, is *Kill Bill*, and a discussion of the two volumes of that title concludes the book.

Reading over what I have written, I find there are a few recurrent topics, and rather than attempt to summarise the individual chapters, it may be more useful to suggest what these topics are and how they are covered.

Characters and types

In Chapter 1 I spend some pages considering the figures that populate Stanley Kubrick's *The Killing* (1956), not especially because it is sometimes quoted as a source for *Reservoir Dogs*, but rather to establish some terms in which the 'doomed caper' crime movie can be read. I am concerned particularly with how the figure of Larry can be understood in the light of the contrast between Tarantino's vision and the accessible fantasies of the fifties America that Kubrick describes. In discussing *Jackie Brown* in the light of Paul Schrader's *Touch* (Chapter 6), I am interested in their versions of the American confidence man, and in *Kill Bill* (Chapter 7) the evident importance of the imagery and meaning of the Western in contemporary America.

Settings: homes and journeys

It should not be surprising to discover how much Tarantino's cinema is concerned with the meanings of settings, who notices them, what is possible in them, and how movements between them are experienced in terms of enchantment or release/rescue. I look at the journeys made by Butch in *Pulp Fiction* and Ordell in *Jackie Brown* in these terms (Chapter 2) and Chapter 5 is devoted to a consideration of different kinds of spaces in all the first three films. In *Kill Bill* (Chapter 7) I have tried to trace the meaning of the heroine's travels, and to relate places to kinds of violence.

Violence

The ear-slicing in *Reservoir Dogs* and the deaths brought about by Vincent and Jules in *Pulp Fiction*, together with their aftermath, are the two prominent occasions of violence that are the subject of the analyses in Chapter 3. The attitude to violence on the part of other individuals is examined in the discussions of Larry (Chapter 1) and Ordell (Chapter 2), and the aesthetics of the photography of different kinds of violence is considered in the context of *Kill Bill* (Chapter 7).

Narrative structures

Tarantino frequently offers narratives in which the chronological order of events has been disturbed. It is one of the most obvious ways in which he can be thought of as a modernist, in the tradition exemplified in Sartre's famous comment on William Faulkner, that he 'did not first conceive this orderly plot so as to shuffle it afterwards like a pack of cards; he could not tell it in any other way' (Jean-Paul Sartre, *Literary and Philosophical Essays*, Hutchinson, 1968, p.79). The examination of the screenplays of *True Romance* and *Natural Born Killers* (Chapter 4) against the films derived from them enables me to consider the meaning of the time schemes in the original writings and the adaptations made on film. The adaptation of an original by another writer is considered in looking at *Jackie Brown* in the light of *Rum Punch*, the novel from which it is derived (Chapter 6), and the structures underlying the complex chronology of *Kill Bill* are probed in Chapter 7.

Endings

So far, Tarantino has shown a marked preference for the less than happy ending. The concluding passages of *Reservoir Dogs* and *Jackie Brown* are partly covered in the first two chapters. The logic and meanings of the films' endings in the light of other, happier versions are examined in the discussions of *True Romance* and *Natural Born Killers* (Chapter 4) and *Jackie Brown* (Chapter 6). In *Kill Bill* (Chapter 7) I attempt to address the paradoxical end to the second part of that film in the light of the earlier discussions.

This book is a critical study of the films and screenplays that I have mentioned. There are, however, several things it makes no claim to be. No part of its intention is biographical, for example, nor am I in a position to give a researched account of the making of the films: the further reading list details work that has already been done in this field. I have also mostly treated Tarantino as if he were solely responsible for what we see on screen – under his name is subsumed the achievement and creative contributions of actors, cinematographers, and technical and production staff. Some part of this problem is always insoluble: again, the further reading list indicates where light is thrown on these collaborations.

Finally, the book is not directed towards the public reception of Tarantino's films, or the mass of material that surrounds them on the Internet. I want my words to take the reader back to the cinema (or maybe to the DVD player). My hope is to be helpful about what Robert Warshow called, in his now happily republished classic of criticism of popular culture, 'the actual, immediate experience of seeing and responding to the movies as most of us see them and respond to them' (author's preface to *The Immediate Experience*, p.xl).

A note on seriousness

Part of what any critic might feel here is 'Oh, not again.' We might recall Robin Wood's view that in 1965 a book on Alfred Hitchcock had to begin with a question about taking Hitchcock seriously, or the later defenders of being serious about, say, *Bonnie and Clyde* or *The Wild Bunch* or David Cronenberg's *Crash*. Whether we are now in a better or worse position to take Tarantino seriously is a larger debate than I can have here (involving as it would a consideration of what forms of humbug can overtake seriousness). It is observable that it is now possible to write seriously and intelligently about a figure from popular cinema who is an acknowledged influence for Tarantino, without having to debate these terms (see Ginette Vincendeau's *Jean-Pierre Melville: An American in Paris*). But that Melville died in 1973, and he was French.

The case of Tarantino suggests that this is an issue that criticism has not answered, but continually finds itself revisiting, particularly as it surfaces through the problematic triangle of the critic, the work and the playful director in interview. There is a suggestive resemblance between some of Hitchcock's comments and some of Tarantino's. (An example: 'To me it's a fun picture . . .', 'I do look at everything as a comedy . . .'. The first is Hitchcock on *Psycho*, the second Tarantino on *Reservoir Dogs*). And to read the objectors to *Psycho* is to realise that the tone remains essentially unchanged – at times they could be writing about *Reservoir Dogs*.

This is not to attempt to compare the two – I am not interested here in where Tarantino comes on a standard set by Hitchcock. Rather, it is to claim that this is work that raises questions of the unreality and reality of violence on the screen and that knows its own comedy. It requires us, maybe as much as work knowing the weight of its own seriousness, to try to express what we can of what its language means. Although this aim cannot be achieved straight away, we may hope that a process of listening and answering will help to elucidate it.

1 Tradition and modernity in *Reservoir Dogs*

[H]is dream must have seemed so close that he could hardly fail to grasp it. He did not know that it was already behind him, somewhere back in that vast obscurity beyond the city.

(F. Scott Fitzgerald (1925), *The Great Gatsby*)

'I did it for money, and for a woman'

(Walter Neff in *Double Indemnity* (Billy Wilder, 1944))

The excitement of approaching Tarantino is an emotion that comes of encountering something new. By this I do not mean to point towards any specific innovation – that would have to be argued and proved – but rather that the films offer an occasion for critical enquiry into something that has not been too thoroughly worked over, that might yet turn out to be gold or dross. In such cases, we have to start out only with the excitement we felt in the cinema, hoping that in interpreting the film we can find grounds to argue for the rightness of our instinct. In trying to turn excitement into an argument, what I have found is that Tarantino's newness can best be understood if we try to see his work in relation to the past of the medium of American film and more broadly of American art. In that respect, I want to claim Tarantino as an American modernist, using the term in the sense defined by Stanley Cavell (1979, p.216), an 'artist whose discoveries and declarations of his medium are to be understood as embodying his effort to maintain the continuity of his art with the art of his past'.

I think that Tarantino invites us, when we explore his contemporary settings, to grasp the continuity between them and the past worlds in which we believe that the values, or fantasies, that are implicit in statements like those quoted at the head of this chapter, could still be asserted. The connection is not a straightforward one: such assertions contain their own recognition of loss, of the impossibility of reconstituting a still earlier, imagined world. Trying to think about these continuities involves

7

considering both the possible decline of those values into something unintelligible, and their persistence.

A way of putting part of this is that an awareness of the absence of something must depend on the sense of its previous presence, or at least on the imagined possibility of that presence. I shall be arguing that what makes Tarantino a significant film-maker is precisely his sense of the absences that structure his (our) world, and his success in expressing this in his films. As it is experienced by his characters from *Reservoir Dogs* to *Kill Bill*, we might describe this as a lack of a sufficiently usable relation, either to a past, or to a person, or to a place that can be called home. Tarantino's achievement is to offer us an experience of contemporary culture that dramatises this situation to a point where we can share it. And the films are interesting and readable (and popular) because, in addressing this absence, they speak to a memory of a presence.

As an initial example of such connections, and in an attempt to trace one of them, I shall begin at what was, for the vast majority of Tarantino's viewers, their own beginning – *Reservoir Dogs*. I want to focus on what I think nobody will dispute is the central matter of its plot, which is the figure of Larry (Harvey Keitel), who is also known as Mr White, and his actions: what he decides to do, what he finds himself doing, what he is unable to do. These actions – rescuing Freddy (Tim Roth), defending him, and killing him in the film's final moment – structure the narrative. I shall be considering how these actions can be interpreted through two, obviously related, forms of male American dreaming: that of intimacy (usually but of course not necessarily with a woman) and that of money, of having enough of it to change your world.

The Killing

First I wish to establish a point of departure. This is a film that has been occasionally quoted as a model for *Reservoir Dogs*, Stanley Kubrick's *The Killing* (1956). *The Killing* is indeed useful for understanding Tarantino's film: it throws light on some important differences. Like Tarantino's, the plot of Kubrick's film is built around a robbery, in this case the stealing of the $2 million take of a big racecourse. The robbery is undertaken by a hetero-geneous group of men, and uses a similar proposition to the later film, that the group who carry out the crime has been brought together for this occasion only. However, unlike *Reservoir Dogs*, not all of them are known to the others even during the process of the robbery itself. The basis of the characterisation of this group, the role that money plays, and the myths of success and failure are suggestively different from those in *Reservoir Dogs*.

At the centre of *The Killing* is the image of the successful heterosexual couple, and the belief that the mistakes or limitations of these lives are about to be erased by the money that seems almost to be in their hands. The benign version of this is the handsome young lovers, Johnny Clay (Sterling Hayden), the acknowledged leader of the conspiracy, and Fay (Coleen Gray). Johnny and Fay believe that the money will transform them from an ex-convict and his girl into a well-heeled couple, literally joining the jet set, descending from an American Airlines flight to Boston. The metamorphosis is imagined almost as a form of marriage: Johnny does not directly propose to Fay (with whom, it is implied in a visual detail of their first sequence, he is already sleeping), but tells her to give up her job: 'Tell them you're getting married.' It is as if escaping with the money can stand in for the marriage: cash becomes a more important element in establishing them as a legitimate couple than any ceremony might be.

Kubrick places alongside this two existing marriages of members of the group. The note of the pathos to which such dreams can be reduced is sounded through the track barman Mike O'Reilly (Joe Sawyer) and his tender treatment of his implicitly terminally ill wife Ruthie (Dorothy Adams), in his promise to her that 'you're going to have a fine house, and doctors that will make you well again'. A different and more violent set of fantasies govern the marriage of track cashier George Peatty (Elisha Cook Jr) to Sherry (Marie Windsor). George's relation to Sherry is one of sexual fixation – undeterred by her aggressive humiliation of him, he is convinced that the promise of riches will revive, or create, her interest in him. But Sherry is trapped between her indifference to George and her anxiety that she will in turn be dumped by her younger lover Val (Vince Edwards). Her response to George's promise of riches is to alert Val to the possibility of taking the money away from the robbers, the twist that destroys the success of the initial heist and results in the deaths of most of the group. This is a common device: an exemplary case of using sexual desire as the anarchic force that explodes the carefully executed robbery is *Rififi* (Jules Dassin, 1954) in which the gift of a single jewel to a woman initiates the chain of events that destroys the gang.

Part of Kubrick's point here may be to contrast the two young couples, presenting commitment and fidelity in Johnny and Fay as against selfishness and indifference in Val and Sherry. But the similarities are perhaps as significant as the differences. From Sherry's dogged attempt to secure Val to Fay's strained words to Johnny, 'I'm no good for anybody else. I'm not pretty and I'm not very smart,' what underlies all these relations, whether benign ones or not, is the sense of desperation, of a set of conditions (of ageing, illness, poverty), which it is almost impossible to imagine truly shaking off. This is a world in which the possibility of (further) disaster is

The handsome couple. In *The Killing* Stanley Kubrick allows the action of Johnny (Sterling Hayden) adjusting his girl Fay's (Colleen Gray) belt to imply that they have recently made love. *Source*: British Film Institute.

omnipresent – success always a fantastic, obligatory dream. Thus men tell women repeatedly that 'Everything is going to be all right, I promise you.' (These are Johnny's words to Fay early in the film; Mike and George later offer versions of this assurance.) The visual image associated with this mood is that of the bed. *The Killing* prominently stages scenes around beds: the florid marital bed in the Peattys' apartment, the sickbed in the

O'Reillys', the bed on which Johnny engages in sexual badinage with Sherry after she is surprised in the act of spying on the men.

The bed is also the setting of another configuration that will be important for *Reservoir Dogs*, that of the male/male couple. The sequence takes place on the very early morning of the robbery. Marvin (Jay C. Flippen), the track bookkeeper and one of the conspirators, is woken by Johnny. Sitting up in bed, he confronts Johnny with his fantasy that the two of them are like father and son, that when the robbery is done they should go off together, that perhaps Fay is the wrong girl for him. Johnny sits on the side of the bed, unreceptive to this essentially American fantasy of two males lighting out for the territory. The cumulative effect is to link myths (of success, release, cure and sexual fulfilment) to images of the present moment and the unavoidable truths they embody, reminding us of the sexual appetite that drives several of these figures and of irreversible conditions of age or illness.

The Killing insistently offers, not remote fantasies, but plans, or projects, addressing relations to actual women in its world and made possible by the (hoped for) actual money. But the women on men's minds can be as important when they are imaginary or marginal as when they are actual. An example of this state is Peckinpah's *The Wild Bunch*, in which for the male group women exist largely only as a memory or a fantasy or, in the episodes with prostitutes, a contact from which nothing can grow. The Bunch acknowledge the expected profits of their robbery as their 'opening for a new territory', but they lack the ability to make anything specific beyond this generalised wish, as opposed to the expectations of the spending of money in specific ways in *The Killing*.

In *Reservoir Dogs* these matters are taken to a further stage. Money, in the sense of the power of money radically to transform a life, is not at issue. Money is thought of by Tarantino's robbers in terms of a reasonable recompense for a job of work. Theft is treated as the work these men do, just as other groups of men herd cattle, or toil in offices or steel mills. It is what they have done before and will do again after the particular instance that is in front of us, as opposed to the idea of the unique heist as exemplified in *The Killing*.

Equally, the presence of women has receded to a remote point, almost disappeared. There are no beds, or couples, no needs. Even the fantasies appear to be largely distanced, attached to figures from pop music, or TV shows. This is as true of the cop as of the robbers. Tarantino carefully avoids the easy sentiment of giving Freddy an explicit or implicit relation to a partner: there is no photograph of a girlfriend. When we see a wedding ring it is one slipped on by Freddy before he goes out to meet the group, not a symbol of union but a theatrical prop. Even such social identity as remains (one of the characters will describe this remnant as your name, where you are from, and what your specialty is) must be disavowed. But of course none of these subjects can be finally erased: an issue of intimacy will determine the trajectory of *Reservoir Dogs* as inevitably as it does in *Rififi* or *The Killing*.

Types of modern life: the soldier

We need to establish a category, or type, that will help us to understand the group in *Reservoir Dogs*. We can certainly say they are not men of power or influence, but neither do they present themselves as a group of renegades. They do not appear to be interested in opposing what they understand society to be, and are happiest when their work seems to disrupt it least, as I shall go on to argue. Their most marked characteristic, considering them as we see them in the pre-credits sequence as they sit around the coffee-shop table, is a degree of variation (age, physical type, involvement in the conversation) that nonetheless observes limits (there is no variation of race or gender). It is contained within an assumed – imposed? – uniformity, literally of clothing, but perhaps less definably of manner, as if they are acting from within a reading of themselves as a type.

I propose that this male group can be thought of as a military one, that the terms in which Tarantino characterises them are essentially those that have constituted a definition of a kind of soldier or military man. I am not suggesting that this category itself is one of which they are aware – rather, the treatment is such as to suggest it to us. I am following here an identification of a type (as opposed to a simple description of an activity) that can be traced back as far as the cultural commentary of Baudelaire, and that has been brought to the attention of film scholars by Stanley Cavell. (See Baudelaire's 'The Soldier' in his 1863 article 'The Painter of Modern Life', and Chapters 7–9 of Cavell's *The World Viewed*.) Consider the following:

1. I have already noted that they are men following careers, rather than engaging in crime as an anomalous or exceptional act. We learn in the course of the film that five of the eight men are experienced criminals and that two, (Joe Cabot (Lawrence Tierney) and Nice Guy Eddie (Chris Penn)), service that criminal activity, that is to say that they do not commit the act of robbery itself, but organise, plan, deal with supplies and communications. Freddy (Mr Orange), the undercover cop, is equally following a pathway within the career to which he is committed.
2. They are men trained to do a job within a team, and not in terms that depend on a social context. We learn that although Joe is known to a few

of them, no individual member of the six is known to any one of the others. Despite this evident lack of relation or shared context, each of them has an exact role in what they are collectively undertaking, an assigned speciality.

3. The community of the military: none of the six are shown as having any connection to the cares or relations of the ordinary world, but rather as being prepared to give over their daily lives, at least for a period, into the hands of the organisation headed by Cabot, who is implicitly supplying them with money and some form of living space in the period of planning the robbery.

4. The relation to violence: they conceive of what they are doing as risky, to be sure, something where the possibility of violence exists but is by no means certain or necessarily desired. (It will emerge in the course of subsequent events that there is an exception to this, Mr Blonde (Michael Madsen).) But they are not terrified of injury or death, which they accept as part of the chances of their work.

5. Continuity: the end result for them will be an interlude of recreation (the few weeks in Hawaii that Joe refers to in the planning meeting) followed by another period of action of essentially the same kind, another job.

6. Uniform: they are identified, and identify each other, by a number of externals – by their conservative dress (donned for their robbery but absent in, for example, the planning session), and the terms in which they refer to another uniformed body of men (cops) and to those caught in the crossfire (civilians).

7. The childlike: 'living as they do in community, like monks and schoolboys . . . soldiers are in many matters as simple as children' (Baudelaire, op. cit.). We can find this element of their interaction in, say, the conversation over Joe's assignment of the pseudonyms in the planning session.

If this definition is felt to be at all helpful, we must bear in mind that we are seeing a particular, extreme version of the type. These men in uniform exist in a context in which there is no cause, local or national, to be defended, or a larger interest to be served. (I think the presentation of Cabot's office is suggestive here, and will return to it in a later chapter.)

Another male group offers a point of reference. Writing about the changing cultures that films address, Robin Wood has argued (in the preface to the second revised edition of *Hitchcock's Films*) that in *Rio Bravo* Howard Hawks rejects 'all the obvious, traditional reasons why its heroes fight: comfort, security, glory, prestige, the acquisition of wealth, the future of civilization'. Wood continues, 'of course, they live (or lived) in a world in which the Burdetts [a corrupt and evil family] could still be defeated'. We can say of the group in *Reservoir Dogs* that of course the same traditional reasons for fighting are not in play, but further that these men (the word heroes being no longer appropriate) live in a world in which nothing hangs on the conflict between them and another body of armed men. The equivalent to the Burdetts can no longer even be identified, let alone defeated. They will kill cops, and cops will kill them, but we are not offered a prospect for either side of final defeat or eventual victory, or a sense of what such terms would mean. Not only are the group largely disconnected from profit and production (as soldiers, rather than workers) but also from any idea of service, despite the claim to act like 'professionals'.

There is one respect in which the group can be distinguished from soldiers as usually conceived. What they lack, apart from the role of Joe, is a sense of command structure derived from rank. What seems to substitute for it, to be one of the factors organising relations within the group and one that determines parts of the action, is familiar from many Westerns – the sense of experience, largely turning on chronological age.

From the very opening of the film, this is unmissable. One of the important visual elements of the pre-credits sequence is the physical appearance of the characters, and the observation that they fall into two broad age groups. The unmistakeably young are made up of the characters played by Roth, Madsen, Tarantino and Penn. Against them stand a group of older men, the characters played by Tierney, Keitel, Bunker and, arguably, Buscemi, who is presented (I suggest not casually) as the one character who is clearly assignable to neither group.

The latter (older) group can be distinguished quite easily, in terms of their access to, and wielding of, authority. Tarantino gives us one figure clearly without it, making no claim to it (Bunker), and one clearly possessing it, the host of the morning and organiser of the robbery (Tierney). This leaves Keitel and Buscemi, and the action in the sequence is organised around two sets of exchanges, one of which demonstrates the possession of authority (Keitel's confiscation and then voluntary return of Tierney's address book), and one of which demonstrates the failure successfully to assert it (Buscemi's attempt to exempt himself from tipping the waitress). Thus, by the end of the pre-credits sequence, a structure has been established that substitutes for military rank.

What is the idea of proper behaviour that applies to such men? Looking over the discussion of the military man as a type in Baudelaire we find 'accustomed as he is to surprises, the soldier does not easily lose his composure', and 'self-reliance and, as it were, a more than ordinary sense of personal responsibility'. So what we might expect to find would be this composure, or the recovery of it when it is lost, the assertion of personal responsibility for one's actions, and self-reliance. We can consider the presence of these qualities in the interaction between Freddy and Larry.

Freddy and Larry

Following what is established in the pre-credits sequence, Tarantino begins the next movement of his film, over the fade to black at the end of the credits, with the sound of screaming. As we cut to the image we find Freddy, who lies bleeding copiously in the back of a getaway car driven by Larry. So there is a passage of (obviously disastrous) events lost to us, or at least not yet explained. It is the kind of disorientation of the viewer of which Tarantino is fond, as if he feels a need to remind us of how often experience offers us material of which we can make initially little or no sense. If we do not know what is going on, no more do they, in the sense that they cannot tell whether Larry will outrun the cops, or whether Freddy will die in the next few minutes. What we share with these characters is the sense of being catapulted into something, without enough data to make firm judgements about actions and their consequences. And what we see is behaviour based on the relation that the two found themselves in earlier, that of the older authority and younger neophyte in the opening. The effect of juxtaposing (by editing that excises the robbery itself) these two temporally separate periods is to emphasise the connection between them.

The relation is presented in the dialogue, as Larry cajoles and bullies Freddy ('Pardon me, I didn't know you had a medical degree . . .'). Freddy's physical condition creates a relation that is almost one of adult to infant, finally confirmed in the line that explicitly acknowledges this in its language: 'Go ahead and be scared, you've been brave enough for one day.'

Why does this act of rescue come to be laden with meaning for Larry, so much so that he will lose his life defending Freddy at the end of the film? My answer is that it comes to express his belief in the possibility of a benign relation to another person (and hence the possibility of such relations for others), which involves an understanding of what such beliefs involve and what they can be opposed to. (The hopes that are fostered in *The Killing* are not in the end so very different from these.)

As the film fills us in on the detail of what happened in the jewellery raid and its immediate aftermath we see an opposition being defined by Larry. On one side there is his sense of proper behaviour, which he calls acting like a 'professional'. This includes what he thinks of as military necessity, shooting cops or shooting a civilian as a deliberate act in order to avoid capture. It also includes looking after your own: succouring the wounded, or making sure that they are beyond help. So we see not only Larry's

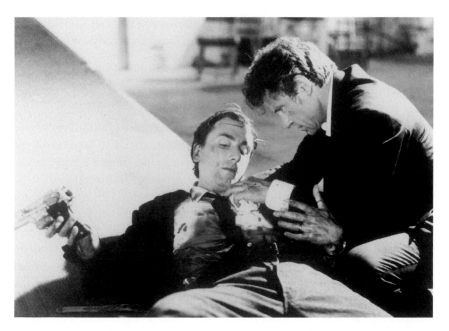

Reservoir Dogs. 'Without medical attention I'm gonna die': the badly injured Freddy (Tim Roth) is comforted by Larry (Harvey Keitel). *Source*: British Film Institute.

rescuing of Freddy from the mayhem that follows the robbery, but checking on Mr Brown (Quentin Tarantino). He asks Freddy twice to confirm that Mr Brown is dead before they abandon him. Larry's expression of this propriety, his justification of his actions to himself, is to assert that the act of rescuing Freddy was a moral consequence, following on from his statement that Freddy's wound was his fault.

It is worth pausing over this claim, for what we see does not exactly confirm it. It would seem more obvious to take the shooting of Freddy by the woman driver as one of the unlucky chances of those desperate minutes, and it is significant that Larry chooses not to see it this way. So what we understand is that Larry wants to accept the blame for Freddy's state, so that he can assert this example of personal responsibility as a way of rhetorically distinguishing himself from the likes of Mr Pink (Steve Buscemi): 'That bullet in his belly is my fault. Now while that might not mean jack shit to you, it means a helluva lot to me.'

The other side of an emerging opposition is embodied in Mr Blonde. It is an attitude that responds to any hostile act by using it as an excuse not just for violence, but specifically to kill, as opposed to the carefully graduated ways of disabling hostility that we hear Larry explain to Freddy in the pre-robbery sequence late in the film, a sequence that seems unimportant until we realise that its point is to set up the attitude to Blonde in the aftermath of the bloodbath at the jewellery warehouse. At issue here is also a fault in military terms, the failure to distinguish between the enemy and civilians, which is a fundamental distinction for both Larry and Mr Pink. Take this exchange (which is a distant echo of the famous moment in Chapter 32 of Mark Twain's *The Adventures of Huckleberry Finn* in which two prominent characters similarly deny the humanity of a whole group):

MR PINK: Tagged a couple of cops. Did you kill anybody?
LARRY: A few cops.
MR PINK: No real people?
LARRY: Uh-uh, just cops.
MR PINK: Could you believe Mr Blonde?

For the two thieves the war with the cops legitimises massive violence in both directions: in their minds both sides regard the other as entirely proper targets, up to and including shooting to kill. We should not, for example, assume that Larry has any humane reaction to the cop captured by Mr Blonde – he is just another hostile, to be beaten and finally executed. But this attitude can – does – go along with a sense of outrage and loss at violence outside those terms, Larry's rules of war. Significantly, he finds himself describing this violence not just through broad terms – 'madman' or 'psychopath' – but through this image: 'I mean, Jesus Christ, how old do you think that black girl was? Twenty, maybe twenty-one?'

Expressed here – not, of course, necessarily consciously – is Larry's sense that the activity of robbery has conventions, and that his self-respect is defined by observing those conventions. I have noted that he does not allow members of his own side to bleed to death in the street or be captured alive by the enemy. In his view the conventions also do not allow the pointless and unnecessary destruction of a civilian life, particularly one that has only a menial connection to the power and money embodied in the diamonds. I suggest this is the point of telling us that the figure is both a young girl and black. (The ground for the moment has been prepared for by Larry's defence of waitresses in the pre-credits sequence.) The girl's death can be offered – as Larry here offers it to Mr Pink – as an unarguable example of vicious and pointless murder.

This opposition can be expressed as the gulf between those who act with regard only to themselves, and those whose acts imply a world of plurality, in which actions are played out in acknowledgement of others and thus include the possibilities of forgiving, promising and revenge. (The classic discussion of this is the chapter entitled 'Action' in Hannah Arendt's *The Human Condition*.) I think this opposition is as much a pressing one to Larry as the question of what actually went wrong with the heist, and an issue that is as real to him as the matter of whether or not one of the group is an undercover cop.

Thus we might characterise Larry as the good soldier, one who comes to the episode of the jewellery raid with a sense of observing the limits and obligations of the military life. Suggestively, he is the only character who specifically alludes to another kind of life, and rejects it with a soldier's stoicism: 'You push it long enough that woman/man thing gets in your way after a while.' (A passage dealing with Joe's marriage in the sequence that includes these words was cut from the completed film.)

It is important that Tarantino states here clearly that Larry has chosen to be alone. The shock, or revelation, of the events of the film is that his action in rescuing Freddy, initiated in the terms I have discussed, suddenly propels him into a form of intimacy, a feeling that the culture that he inhabits is designed to repress or deny. There are the literals of this intimacy: Larry cradling Freddy in his arms, dabbing his forehead, combing his hair. The fact that these take place in a welter of Freddy's blood seems to be Tarantino's way of prompting a reading of how this unlooked-for closeness affects Larry – that he is marked, literally stained by it, connected to Freddy in a way that he cannot erase. But we might also say, this is *only* blood, staining but conferring no real knowledge. We should also note that the possibility that Freddy might be imminently dying cuts across the military discipline of formal (and disguising) nomenclature, so that Larry tells Freddy his first name.

What follows from this is a significant moment. In his conversation with Mr Pink Larry rails on the convention of withholding names within the group of thieves. Tarantino writes the speech so that Larry suddenly generalises, seeing the issue as representative of a larger culture in which no form of plurality can be achieved: 'What the fuck was I supposed to tell him: "Sorry, I can't give out that information . . .".'

The final element that binds Freddy and Larry, and simultaneously places them apart from Joe and Nice Guy Eddie, is their relation to Mr Blonde. In killing Mr Blonde, and thus enacting what Larry said earlier that he wanted to do, Freddy both completes Larry's desire and associates himself with Larry's judgement of Blonde. This again underlines that the division is not between cop and robbers but between those who possess a belief in a world of plurality and those who lack it.

At the climax of the action the value of intimacy – the assertion, the loss, the existence of it – is very much the central element. There is the assertion, on Larry's part, that the contact between himself and Freddy must confer knowledge, just as it has transferred blood – his desperate cry of 'I know this man . . .'. Nicely juxtaposed with this by Tarantino is the one actual blood relationship in the plot, the feeling that produces Eddie's terrified shout of 'Stop pointing that fucking gun at my dad' just before the shooting starts.

Engaging with tradition

Tarantino addresses a world defined by strategies that operate to keep people at a distance from each other. These strategies have become internalised to the point that friendship can only take the form of uneasy horseplay: see the first re-encounter of Eddie and Mr Blonde, for example. For Larry, the world is exploded by his sudden, shocking projection into a relation of intimacy with another.

Intimacy becomes confused with true knowledge of the other, and the consequences of this confusion are absolutely destructive. It is worth noting that the plot in which a man who prides himself on a kind of coolness or cynicism towards others falls vertiginously into what he thinks of as an intimate relationship that proves totally destructive is not new. It is familiar where the players are a heterosexual couple. It is, for example, an element of *Double Indemnity*, where again one of the couple will feel the call to shoot the other in the end.

Thus Larry, who has by his own account turned away from some of the routes of desire that inform American fantasies and perhaps sees himself more in tune with (or protected from) modern culture by so doing, finds himself in a relationship that he does not expect, but in which he finds that he believes. The significance, not of dying, but of something that must be transmitted at the moment in which dying is being contemplated – 'I mean, the man was dying in my arms' – comes to substitute for the loss or abandonment of other kinds of closeness. We find that the configuration of the dying soldier and his comrade in arms, viewed as an image of the asserted significance of relations between men, will appear again in *Pulp Fiction*.

In *Reservoir Dogs* Tarantino places a familiar configuration in a new context. When Larry says, 'You push it long enough that woman/man thing gets in your way after a while,' he is giving expression to a male aversion to women that can be traced through characters played in some of their films by (say) Clint Eastwood and Gary Cooper, themselves the inheritors of the literary tradition that stretches back through Twain and Melville. It has been widely argued, definitively by Leslie Fiedler in his *Love and Death in the American Novel*, that an element in this mythology is the non-sexual bond between male and male, sometimes explicitly between those who meet across sides of a racial divide. (Famous cases of this in American literature are Leatherstocking and Chingachook in James Fenimore Cooper's cycle of 'Leatherstocking' novels, Ishmael and Queequeg in Melville's *Moby-Dick*, Huck and Jim in Twain's *The Adventures of Huckleberry Finn*. In film the male/male couple appears in many Westerns, *films noirs*, prison melodramas and detective/police plots. John Dunbar (Kevin Costner) and Kicking Bird (Graham Greene) in *Dances with Wolves*, and William Munny (Clint Eastwood) and Ned Logan (Morgan Freeman) in Eastwoood's *Unforgiven* are two exemplary cases from the 1990s.)

The place to which Tarantino takes this is to give us the male/male couple literally bathed in blood, and the racial difference is transformed into that of the difference between thief and cop. The impossibility of sustaining the bond is commonly expressed by one of the couple dying: here both parties will die in the closing seconds.

2 Success and failure in *Pulp Fiction* and *Jackie Brown*

The initial contact between the film and its audience is an agreed conception of human life: that man is a being with the possibilities of success or failure. This principle, too, belongs to the city; one must emerge from the crowd or else one is nothing.

> (Robert Warshow (1962), 'The Gangster as Tragic Hero'
> in *The Immediate Experience*)

Butch Coolidge (Bruce Willis) from *Pulp Fiction* and Ordell Robbie (Samuel L. Jackson) from *Jackie Brown* represent extremes of success and failure from Tarantino's work. Butch is an obvious choice as a success in that he is one of the few important male characters who survives the action of the film and ends his part with the promise of a future. Ordell is a significant figure in that the qualities and limitations that destroy him are signalled almost from the beginning. I shall be suggesting that the trajectories of both figures are determined by situations that are part of long traditions in American culture: in Butch's case by his relation to fatherhood, and in Ordell's case by the different terms in which he relates to men and to women.

Out of the past: Butch Coolidge and the fathers' watch

The situation of Butch Coolidge can be distinguished from those of the other main figures in *Pulp Fiction* in one respect, which also distinguishes him from the characters in *Reservoir Dogs*. This can be expressed in terms of visions of the future. It can be said of the other characters in both films that they suppose that twelve months' time will find them in much the same roles and occupations as the present – they do not anticipate changing their lives in any radical way. (This distinction is, of course, not contradicted by the actual course of events, in which some of them die, or undergo a transformation – I am thinking here of their expectations.)

The evident difference in Butch's situation is marked perhaps by stillness, the long take (about 90 seconds, without camera movment) that introduces him, lit from the side in such a way as to give his face a Janus-like character. The monologue, something like the delivery of a judgment, is spoken by Marcellus Wallace (Ving Rhames), the millionaire gangster who sits opposite him. It is marking a pivotal moment in Butch's life, which we learn is that of a professional boxer. It is the point at which the logic of events dictates that he should throw a fight, collect a substantial payment, and leave the business. This logic is based on a view of Butch's physical state that goes unchallenged: that he has 'ability', but that his ability has peaked. If he were going to be a champion, it would have happened by now. So we appear to be beginning with a story of failure, or acknowledgement of the end of a dream.

The way Tarantino shoots the sequence, giving us no frontal view of Marcellus and thus no sense that Butch is exactly looking at him, emphasises the quality of the moment as one in which Butch is not being told something new or unexpected, but facing a truth of which he is already aware. His relation to the moment is possibly not so much one of acknowledging that he will throw this specific fight as of admitting that his successes in the ring are now part of the past.

There is also an issue of power here. The terms in which Butch is positioned, as a functionary whose value to Marcellus is his implicit absolute obedience, a figure who exercises his masculinity entirely under direction, characterises them less as boss and worker than as master and slave. This is underlined by the difference in race of the two characters (ironically challenging expectations, with the subservient character here being the white one). It also has the effect of removing any suggestion that Marcellus is in a fatherly role to Butch. The reasons for this, or rather the importance of it, will become evident in due course.

The interview with Marcellus concludes, and a version of Butch's future now seems to be sketched, in the otherwise strangely unmotivated hostile exchange with Vincent (John Travolta) at the bar of the nightclub in which these events are taking place. The insult is to call Butch 'punchy'. Again, his response includes a quality of contemplativeness, as if he is thinking not just how to respond to Vincent, but what it might be like to become a has-been.

We next see Butch – much later, after the film's long passage with Mia (Uma Thurman) and Vincent – in something that is between a dream and a memory. This is the sequence set in 1972, when the 5-year-old Butch (Chandler Lindauer) faces another figure, this one much more like a father,

Captain Koons (Christopher Walken), who has come to deliver to him his father's watch. The lighting of the child's face, again illuminated from the side, links the figure with the contemplative adult of the earlier sequence.

The point of Koons' account of the watch (purchased by Butch's great-grandfather, transmitted through the next three generations from fathers to sons) seems easy to grasp. It speaks to an idea of male duty (the Coolidge men going off to war) culminating in sacrifice (the two who die respectively in combat and in a prison camp). It repeats a highly specific configuration: that of the father being at the point of death and entrusting the watch to an agent-figure, named in the narrative, to pass on to the son he has never seen. Thus this moment, Koons' visit to Mrs Coolidge (Brenda Hillhouse) and her infant son, has its precedent in Gunner Winocki's act: 'he paid a visit to your grandmother, delivering to your infant father his dad's gold watch'. Of the two roles, that of the patriarch (the donor of the watch) is flexible, can be transferred from one man to another, but that of the son (the receiver of the watch) is fixed. It can change only when the son becomes a father and in turn bequeaths the watch to his son.

The act of transmission celebrates a relation of trust between men. It speaks to keeping your word to the dead comrade and to acknowledging that in circumstances of violent change, of death in a remote place, it is possible to preserve a talismanic object. The continuity between the

Pulp Fiction. The delivery of an object and of a narrative: Captain Koons (Christopher Walken) tells the story of the fortunes of the family gold watch to the infant Butch. *Source*: British Film Institute.

moments in which the watch is handed on implies the continuity of the belief in the significance of such moments: we might say, a belief in significance itself. A wedding ring, which might speak to uniqueness of a given couple, is a rather different object. Closer to this case is the bracelet passed from party to party in Howard Hawks' *Red River*, which represents, I think, the belief in the possibility of human society in the face of the forces that operate to disrupt it in that film.

As this sequence ends, we cut to the adult Butch, alone in the locker room immediately before the fight that he has been told to throw. Tarantino's liking for omitting the social event, the piece of work, and concentrating on the worlds either side of it, is in play here, as we cut from the moment before the fight to its aftermath. We learn that Butch is indeed accepting that this is his final fight, but in terms opposite to those dictated by Marcellus. He intends to ignore their deal, and has laid bets on himself to win. He will dash away at the end of the fight, meet his girl, and flee with her, first to the South, in order to collect the money he has won, and then to the Carribean or similar, somewhere that he hopes will be out of reach of these gangsters.

We see the difference between the kinds of choices made in Butch's current world and the choices that presented themselves to the past generations of Coolidge men. The note of consistency or repetition (of valour, of sacrifice) has no easy relation to Butch's life. I think an awareness of this is behind the way in which Butch's memory of Koons is positioned by Tarantino: we see it presented as a dream out of which he wakes with a shout of stress, or shock. This does something more than a dissolve would have done, in establishing the story as something that is both intimately part of Butch's psyche and something he cannot understand, or know how to respond to. Some psychic process that the watch represents has come to a halt, or become suspended. Butch has no son, which is a way of saying that he is still the fatherless son of the moment of his memory of Koons. The consequence is that there is no opportunity for the ritual transmission of the precious object, and thus no way in which its significance can be affirmed.

In order to read the way in which Butch will solve this problem, it is necessary to notice several elements of the way that Tarantino presents him. One is the recurrent image of his waking and falling asleep (or losing consciousness and regaining it). Another is his shift of attention from the world on the television screen to the world outside it, which we see in the opening of the Koons sequence and the morning sequence in the motel with his girl Fabienne (Maria de Medeiros). What these suggest is a character whose movements between real and imagined worlds are sufficiently frequent, and in some cases unexpected, as to make it difficult to distinguish them, or easy to confuse them.

If there are hints of this quality in the Koons sequence, they become explicit in the passage of Butch's flight, which takes us from the end of the boxing match to his arrival at the motel where Fabienne is waiting for him. Notice the following:

1. that the break with the past, and with Marcellus, is represented not just in the defeat of the other boxer, but the (seemingly unlikely) fact of his death;
2. that when a taxi arrives it is driven by a beautiful woman, with a name from fantasy ('one hell of a name', in Butch's words), Esmerelda Villa Lobos (Angela Jones);
3. the visual detail, hardly more than a flash insert, of Esmerelda's *naked* foot on the pedal of the car;
4. finally, the much more prominent use of a visual device, and so more directly requesting our thought about it. This is the fact that the back-projection of the LA streets as we see them through the windows of the car is in black and white.

What this seems to be doing is more than just finding a way of expressing Butch's euphoria, his sense of release from the bond of the past, the slave's flight to a new world. He experiences his moment of flight as one in which the past is dead (the opponent's death), a new existence in which ordinary or routine presences become extraordinary (the beauty of a random taxi driver), and in which the ordinary, or the place in which he has spent his old life, becomes remote (the black-and-white back-projection). This is, then, a passage of enchantment, when the world seems to conform to the expectations of fairy tale, in which the being that whisks Butch from one world to another is shoeless, not quite of the earth.

But only briefly so. What Tarantino now does is to return Butch to the ordinary (or possibly to locate him in it firmly for the first time?), in the form of the motel room he shares with Fabienne. From a world of enchantment we are suddenly plunged into one of something that re-sembles marital intimacy, as the couple prepare to make love (in the sense that their conversation is leading in that direction). They are thinking about their future: they talk, make love, wake up, quarrel over his teasing her.

What interrupts these ordinary events is another moment of Butch's startled waking, as he sits up in bed with a shout that recalls the end of the Koons sequence. Here what seems to have prompted the shock is not a memory but a movie, the one that is playing on the motel TV, which Fabienne refers to as a 'motorcycle movie', but about which Butch notices the 'explosions and war'. We now briefly see an image of the TV screen, from Butch's point of view, in which a miniature figure of Fabienne

Pulp Fiction. The ordinary intimacies of lovers assert themselves as Fabienne (Maria de Medeiros) enquires of Butch (Bruce Willis), 'Will you give me oral pleasure?'
Source: British Film Institute.

(supposedly reflected on the glass surface of the tube) is juxtaposed with the mayhem of the war movie. The figures are disposed so that Fabienne seems to stand apart from the image in the movie – Butch sees into the screen, to this action, and Fabienne remains on the sidelines. The image crystallises for a moment the quality of Butch's consciousness that I have tried to describe, in which fantasy (tales of past wars) and reality (this actual woman) interpenetrate.

The image introduces the next movement of their story, in which it emerges that in abandoning their apartment Fabienne forgot to bring the father's watch. When his rage and panic subsides, Butch admits (essentially talking to himself) that he had not told her the watch was the only thing of importance to him in the place. Why not? It is not hard to see that in making a break into a new life, part of what Butch unconsciously wanted might have been to leave the watch behind. But this itself is equally the subject of two opposed motivations. One is to abandon the past, the scenario that the watch represents. The other is to have created precisely the situation where he must go back for the watch. It is the latter that he finds now that he wants.

It may be helpful now to sum up the remaining action of Butch's story, before commenting on it. He returns to the apartment to retrieve the watch, and does so. The place is being guarded by Vincent – by a stroke of good luck, Butch defeats and kills him. He is returning to collect Fabienne when, completely by chance, he encounters Marcellus. He tries to disable him and escape, but fails; the two engage in a struggle in which Marcellus tries to kill Butch, but it is not quite clear what Butch wants. Rather than simply trying to escape, he ambushes Marcellus in a pawnshop, and seems intent on beating him, but it is not clear that he will, or can, kill him. At this point they are both taken prisoner by the owner of the shop, and taken to a basement that is a place of abuse and rape, where it is implied they will both be tortured and finally killed. Marcellus is raped. Butch escapes as far as the threshhold but returns to rescue Marcellus, and the final bargain between the two men involves the granting to Butch of his freedom from pursuit. He collects Fabienne and the couple leave for Tennessee, in what is chronologically the end of Tarantino's movie, a happy ending tucked neatly away in the centre of the film.

Let us take the matter of the watch first. My argument is that Butch is one of a long line of American figures defined in part by the absence or death of the father. This presents the familiar conflict between the possibility of being free of the weight of the past and its values, and the loss of identity, the danger of finding yourself in a world in which you have no purpose, nothing to inherit. (A useful summary of this subject is to be found in Raymond Carney's book (1986, pp.40–5) on Frank Capra.) Butch can neither continue to be permanently in the position of the aspiring son, nor can he allow himself to assume the role of the father. The function of the earlier conversation in the motel between Fabienne and Butch on the subject of pot bellies is to make this fairly explicit. Fabienne's yen for a pot belly seems to be an obvious coding for raising the subject of pregnancy, and Butch's response at this point is to reject it: 'I would punch you in your pot belly.'

Thus he cannot abandon the watch, and he cannot simply take it with him (as he could have done, to the fight). He has to create the situation where he will rescue it, in circumstances of great danger, a ritual in which he can receive the watch a second time. Thus Butch here is both the party who takes great risks to deliver the talismanic object, thus acknowledging its significance, and the party to whom the object is transmitted. (Or transmitted again – Freud's formulation that the finding of something is always the re-finding of it comes to mind here.) By short-circuiting the difference between the fathers (or their representatives) and the sons, he frees himself of the sense of being trapped in the role of the childless orphan.

This moment of psychic release is followed by the descent of Butch and Marcellus as captives into a kind of underworld, a place of pain and torture, where for the first time they are entirely equal (their torturer has some difficulty deciding which of them he is going to torment first). After Butch has escaped there is the moment of decision, the shot of him poised on the threshold of the pawnshop, deciding to rescue Marcellus, and then the sequence in which he exercises another kind of choice (of the weapon he will take back with him to the underworld). It is tempting to see this, in the light of the events surrounding the watch, as Butch's opportunity to express comradeship, to perform a further rescue. Is Tarantino saying this, as he poses Butch in the doorway, against the background of the American flag (and the Tennessee licence plate, a small reminder of Butch's future plans)? It is worth noting that the image is what we see, not what Butch, whose back is to the flag and plate, is necessarily aware of. It may be rather that Tarantino wants to allow the association to be made only indirectly, to pun on the notion that a view of fighting for America is Butch's psychic inheritance, one that is literally behind him here. And he may be conscious that the gesture, the moment of return to the fray, is now ironically inflected: the rescue of this gangster from these psychopaths.

Certainly it is important, and typical, that Butch does not provide a rationale for his actions – they are as spontaneous as Larry's rescue of Freddy in *Reservoir Dogs*. Butch treats the rescue as a ritual (we might assume that ritual has been important to his role as a prizefighter). What becomes the expressed and conscious choice is not whether he should rescue Marcellus, but his selection of a weapon. The final choice is of the ritual weapon, the Japanese sword, chosen over hammer, baseball bat and chainsaw.

Finally there is another American image, the conferring of freedom upon a slave, in the matter of Butch and Fabienne's release from LA. In the film's world, flight, as Butch imagines it, can no longer confer freedom, as there is no longer a part of the world into which the operations of a Marcellus do not reach. (Marcellus' business is defined as international through Vincent's first conversation with Jules (Samuel L. Jackson) – also the first statement when Marcellus discovers that Butch has not thrown the fight: 'If Butch goes to Indo-China, I want a nigger hidin' in a bowl of rice, ready to pop a cap in his ass.') Freedom has to be granted by Marcellus; it is both a reward for his rescue and the price of Butch's silence (about Marcellus' rape in the basement). It expresses not intimacy but almost its opposite, the erasure of any relation between the two men. When Butch asks Marcellus, 'What about you and me?', at first he is misunderstood, and the reply is then 'There is no you, and there is no me.' In the screenplay, Tarantino has the two men embrace as they part. In the film, the final shot of Marcellus in this segment shows him with his back to Butch and to the camera, one hand raised in salute and dismissal. (It can be related back to the final couple of *Reservoir Dogs* – there the two men dead, here the two dead to each other.)

What is left for Butch is the reinsertion into the mundane world, as he clumsily tries to hurry Fabienne up so that they do not miss their connection for Knoxville. Perhaps the character of Butch is interesting to Tarantino because he experiences the world both as myth, as a tale of enchantment and release, and as a literal world of objects and discriminations. The two sides are represented here in their final scene – the escape from the past in the pronouncement of the death of the figure of mythical threat ('Zed's dead'), and the literal distinction between a chopper and a motorcycle that Butch patiently makes to Fabienne in their final moments on screen. Such issues matter to him because they are both significant ways of grasping the world.

Ordell in *Jackie Brown*

Ordell and men

All of the strands of the narrative of *Pulp Fiction* are in various respects related to the status of Marcellus Wallace, which Tarantino in the screenplay describes as like a 'king'. We see a world driven by Marcellus' money, and the quality of his authority is frequently expressed not by any direct action on his part but through his subordinates, and the assumption that Jules and Vincent, Butch, even the Wolf, will do his bidding without question. (Although this proves untrue in the case of Butch, the betrayal confirms how strong the assumption is, in that nobody for one moment contemplates the possibility that he might renege on a deal with Marcellus.) It is also implicit that Marcellus' financial interests are sufficiently extensive for no one deal – not the money laid out on Butch, nor the contents of the briefcase that Jules retrieves – to affect them seriously. This sense of extent is mirrored in the idea of geographical reach denoted by Vincent's stories of his time in Europe: Marcellus' network is evidently part of a global operation.

A very different sense of relation to money and geography operates in *Jackie Brown*. In that arms dealer Ordell Robbie makes money from a form of crime, he is in a line that can be traced forward from Joe Cabot through Marcellus. But unlike them, he is not the head of a substantial organisation. He is an apparently successful middleman in a world of arms dealing that extends beyond his knowledge or reach and is personified in the Mr Big, called here Mr Wilson, who is on the end of a telephone line but who we never see. Where Joe and Marcellus have their operations, Ordell has one young operative, Beaumont (Chris Rock), and at the point at which the narrative of *Jackie Brown* opens is just initiating an old partner, Louis Gara (Robert De Niro), four days out of jail, into the arms business. And the geography here expresses not a global operation but one in which national borders are a restrictive presence. Most of Ordell's money (and hence his future power and control) is at a problematic remove, in Mexico. Thus he is aware that his success is only contingent, depending on a few last deals to complete his career. He tells Louis that he will then 'spend the rest of my life spending'.

We shall see that Ordell's success, his self-esteem, depends on those parts of the world he knows and understands and is able to manipulate. His destruction is brought about by those he does not. In many respects he is a classic American hero in that part of what he understands is dealings with other men, and part of what he does not is to do with women.

Let us start by taking Ordell at his most successful, in a first encounter with another man whom he wishes to use as a functionary. He wants to impress, to feel his own success and power reflected back in that man's dealings with him, which is the main way in which he preserves and cultivates his sense of self-esteem. The man is Max Cherry (Robert Foster), the bail bond agent to whom Ordell has come in order to organise a bond for Beaumont. The sequence is typical of a kind of scene Tarantino seems greatly to enjoy, in which character and hence the possiblities of plot are elegantly expressed through conversation and its inflections, on topics that might not seem immediately relevant, a little like the sequences in classic *film noir* in which the client arrives in the office of the private eye.

Here the sequence begins with a direct and simple matter of power, Ordell's assertion of his right to smoke, the lack of an ashtray making the gesture the more pointed. Max is unfazed – his position, that of the man who deals with the underworld but who sits behind a desk for now, is that he has seen plenty of Ordells before, that this act isn't about to impress him.

As soon as Ordell enters the room he begins glancing at the framed photographs on the office wall: Tarantino shows us the gesture four times. They are mostly of sporting pursuits, suggesting simply that the man behind the desk is at home in such contexts. Ordell's eye lights on one image, set apart in that it is in colour and a close two-shot, of Max and a heavy-set black figure. The dialogue that follows establishes that the figure, Winston (Tommy 'Tiny' Lister Jr), works with Max, and that Max is his boss.

ORDELL (*in close-up*): Bet it was your idea to take that picture, wasn't it?

(*Tarantino cuts sharply to a close-up of Max, and then cuts immediately to medium shot as Max clears his throat and returns to the subject of the bail bond.*)

The moment is exemplary of Ordell's acuteness in such areas. His hazarding that it was Max's choice to have the picture taken with Winston is a way

of suggesting, if not quite accusing him of, the conventionality of his relation to Winston, as being subject to drives to do with power, colour, phys-
icality and youth, that he has perhaps not had to acknowledge until they are
being gently probed here. Max makes no answer: the issue is not whether
Ordell's speculation is right or wrong, but the easy confidence it demonstrates – his feeling that he has a right to make it, to tease Max a little with it.

The sequence deals with the business of the setting up of the bail bond,
but what we have also understood is Ordell's view of himself – his sense of
being as competent at what he does, and a lot richer, than the man
opposite. In part this is conveyed in performance, in Ordell's body language
in the room, but two further dialogue exchanges (the later one concluding
the sequence) are exemplary.

MAX: Would you say Beaumont is his first or his last name?
ORDELL: I would say Beaumont is his Christian name.

MAX (*of Ordell's address*): Is that an apartment or a house?
ORDELL (*with a clear, satisfied emphasis on the last word*): That's a house.

Ordell's confidence, we might say his charm, in dealing with men (and
the adeptness with which he organises a discourse around racial difference
or similarity) are strikingly shown off again in the sequence that immediately follows, the execution of Beaumont. It seems that the sequence is
almost included to demonstrate it: rather than have Ordell simply use a
silencer and shoot Beaumont at his apartment door, we have a long passage
involving Beaumont agreeing to hide in the trunk of Ordell's car, with the
result that he can be driven to another place to be shot. Tarantino offers
some ominous visual information: Ordell's black costume and the hard,
metallic colours, such as the shot of the light falling on the road surface just
before Ordell drives off to carry out the execution. Against this is, of course,
the comedy of the dialogue, in which Beaumont is charmed, manipulated
and bullied into the trunk, evidently without the slightest sense that he is at
risk. The absolute firmness of purpose at this point, Ordell's efficiency as
the killer of another man, is very neatly captured in the camera movement
that includes the execution. The car drives off in medium shot, and instead
of following it or cutting to another set-up, the take continues with a slow
camera movement to the left. It is as if the deliberation of that movement
expresses Ordell's certainty as to what he is doing and why and how: the
image comes to rest on waste ground so that the car in due course can
reappear in the frame, in the place chosen for the execution.

Beaumont's execution is a situation in which no woman is present or
invoked. There appears to be no girlfriend at his apartment, and even on his

TV the image is of a man talking (about his need for a beautiful woman, but there is no woman on the screen with him). Searching around for a treat with which to bribe Beaumont into the trunk, Ordell comes up with food rather than sex. This note of the absence of women will be continued in the final sequence in this group.

Ordell considers that Beaumont's corpse has one last use, as a way of impressing Louis. (I shall discuss Louis in greater detail shortly, but it may be worth observing here that this seems an unlikely piece of reasoning on Ordell's part. Louis' loyalty isn't at all in doubt, so the possibility exists that showing the corpse to him is a piece of boasting, or ritual.) Louis is staying with Simone (Hattie Winston), one of the women that Ordell has installed in properties he owns or controls.

As the sequence of Beaumont's execution concludes, Tarantino cuts to a tight, almost grotesque, close-up of Simone's face. She is putting on a show for Louis, performing a Supremes number in karaoke. Ordell arrives at the house and parks outside. He could go to the door and summon Louis, but he does not do even this. Preferring to telephone from his car, he refuses the invitation to join Simone: 'I caught that act before.' Louis comes out to the car to be confronted with the corpse of Beaumont, and Ordell's gloss on him: 'an employee I had to let go'. The assertion of control juxtaposed with the absence or exclusion of women is consistent with the previous scenes. There is no reason to suppose that Ordell is consciously aware of this. Rather the opposite: the assumptions and conditions that underlie his behaviour are inaccessible to him, and this will prove crucial to his fate in the film, as I shall be going on to argue.

Ordell at home: the beach house

All of the sequences that I have discussed so far are already operating in contrast to the early scene in which Ordell is introduced to the viewer, and in which we see him with a woman, and in something that loosely qualifies as a home. This is an important setting in the film, one to which we return several times, the beach house in which Ordell has installed another of his women, Melanie (Bridget Fonda), a white 'beach bunny'. It is here that the sequence takes place that introduces us to these two, and to Louis. It opens with the image of the television showing a (spoof) programme, *Chicks who Love Guns*. Louis and Ordell are sitting in front of the television, on a sofa; Melanie is sprawled over a chair at right angles to them, so that Louis is situated between her and Ordell.

The sequence could be aligned with the coffee house sequence of *Reservoir Dogs* in that a great deal of the tensions, aversions and energies that will animate the rest of the narrative are on display in it, and being carefully articulated for us. Initially what Tarantino does with this sequence is to use it to 'make us aware that there are two subjects in play – sexual desire and guns – but not equally present for the three characters. For Ordell, the different guns displayed on the television screen are prompts for his boasting about his arms deals. He seems not to notice, or to think worth comment, that the guns are fired by girls in bikinis. Melanie, bored and scornful of Ordell's supposed expertise, makes only one comment on the images on the screen, about the 'chick', not the gun. When she sees a brunette on the screen she smiles at a fancied resemblance and offers: 'Demi Moore!' Between the two, in more than just the matter of his physical position, is Louis. Tarantino shoots the scene so as to emphasise Louis' uneasy awareness of Melanie's body, with close-ups of her foot, adorned with rings, next to his drink, and shots that emphasise his view of her bare legs. Ordell's relation to the spectacle of Melanie's body is to ignore it, to treat Melanie only as a waitress or servant.

We could sum up by saying that the sequence establishes the three principals as follows:

1. Ordell wants Louis to admire his arms dealing, and he wants Melanie to be admired as a trophy. Like the beach house itself and its fittings, he considers that her presence is expressive of his success in life. He expects

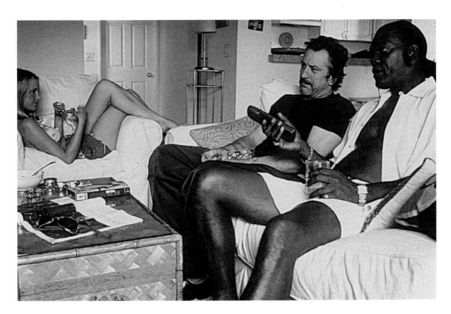

Jackie Brown. Tarantino mapping the tensions within a domestic world: Louis Gara (Robert de Niro) sits uneasily between Melanie (Bridget Fonda) and Ordell Robbie (Samuel L. Jackson). *Source*: British Film Institute.

Melanie to act uncomplainingly in roles that spring, in his mind, from her being his possession. When she is reluctant or uncooperative his only response is mute appeal, or direct aggression. He cannot see that the charm that he exercises on, say, Max or Beaumont has any relevance to dealing with Melanie, and assumes that her behaviour will be controlled adequately by violence, or the threat of it. He is conscious of her sexual desirability but mainly in that her attractiveness, and whiteness, is felt to increase her value as a trophy. He is, and remains (we shall return to this), strongly attached to relations to women that depend on his belief in his domination of them, and his sense of their consciousness of this. This is less a matter of direct sexual domination than one of fear of physical violence.

2. Melanie is entirely uninterested in the arms-dealing business except in so far as it supports her. She is aware of Ordell's evaluation of her, and her response to his demands, as for instance in their spat over answering the telephone, is also aggressive, as if she calls his bluff. She recognises the limited range of his reactions to her, knowing that his only option is to threaten her. She knows that violence would operate against his interests – would degrade the value of his trophy woman – if he were to carry it through. She is well aware that her status in this context depends on her desirability.

3. In the screenplay of *Jackie Brown* Tarantino says of Louis that 'in the real world his timing is thrown'. His responses – attraction to Melanie, being impressed by Ordell – are articulated by De Niro's performance as being contained inside a deep abstractedness, the impression that prison has left him with a consciousness that can relate only to immediate sensations and the objects in front of it. He would be melancholy if the word did not perhaps imply some depth – what we see is possibly better termed sadness.

What links the three figures together is their mutual isolation. What is obvious in Louis, in that it is expressed in a performance of disconnectedness, is concealed in Melanie and Ordell. Both have a view of the world in which their interaction with others is determined by their individual (sexual or physical) dominance or power, and in the end what betrays them is their inability to see that this has limits, that there could be situations not determined by it. We might think forward to the denouement and notice that what links the deaths of all three of the players in the beach house is the quality of surprise. In each case they have willingly entered into a situation that they believe they can control: Melanie teasing Louis in the car park, Louis explaining to Ordell in the camper van, Ordell meeting Jackie in a darkened room. They can be killed in such circumstances exactly because they lack the ability to imagine the possibility of such an event.

Ordell and women

In the light of the sequences that I have discussed so far it is unsurprising that Ordell's first serious error of judgement occurs with a woman. He goes to the apartment rented by Jackie Brown (Pam Grier) intent on attacking her, but she disarms and threatens to shoot him. The differences between the treatment of the two figures whose knowledge of the arms-dealing operation threaten Ordell – Beaumont and Jackie – are expressive. Beaumont was shot outside, after being stuffed into a space that associates him with rubbish, an object to be dumped. Ordell intends to murder Jackie, and imagines it as a kind of extension of the scenario of his supposed control of women. He plans to kill her in her apartment, at night, with his hands rather than a weapon. His assumption, that this way of treating her is the appropriate one, betrays him, creating the conditions (the dark, her space) in which Jackie can pull a gun on him.

This error on Ordell's part is also part of a larger picture of his relations to women and their space. We know from early on that he sets up women in houses or apartments, and as the film develops this configuration recurs in a way that invites the viewer to see it as more than casual. The movement is from the woman and house as trophies, to woman and space as expressive of disgust; the trajectory extends from Melanie and the beach house, to Simone and her place (in which Louis is staying), to Sheronda (Lisa Gay Hamilton), a lost girl from the South that Ordell found at a bus stop, and finally to the unnamed 'glassy-eyed black female junkie' (Tarantino's description of the character in the screenplay) who is a presence in the last, filthy apartment to which Ordell retreats shortly before his death. The argument that the women and these places simply express Ordell's success or power, which has some weight in the case of Melanie or even Simone, begins to need rethinking in the case of Sheronda – what exactly does Ordell need her for? – and the junkie. It is not hard to see that the relation to a woman Ordell can best bear is where the figure is a part of the furnishing of the place, an expression of his spending power. But to repeat this configuration over and over in these various forms is a way of obliterating the uniqueness of any one case of it, as if it is the individuality of these women that is most deeply threatening. Whatever his relation to a woman, from desire to disgust, Ordell wants to impose the same shape and terms on it.

Jackie does not fit sufficiently into the pattern. While Ordell obviously pays her for her services in moving his money, she is not one of the women set up in a place he has provided. In the first sequence with Max in her home, the stress on the personal – her objects, photographs and records – is a way of making this distinction clear to us. (Compare the stack of identical boxes, presumptively stolen goods, in Simone's apartment.)

But if we can see the distinction, Ordell cannot. We may express his problem in the latter half of *Jackie Brown* by saying that he is trapped inside a mental world in which, although Jackie is not one of his kept women, he has no alternative way of thinking of her, or of predicting or judging her behaviour. His belief that she *must* be acting in his interests, and that her dominant emotion with regard to him *must* be fear of what he will do to her, survives his bungled execution attempt and all the slowly developing ramifications of the plotting regarding money exchange that follow. When he spots Max meeting Jackie in the Del Amo Mall, while uneasily recognising that he no longer dictates events, Ordell cannot revise his vision usefully. He cannot respond to his sense of the plot unravelling because he cannot imagine a scenario that allows for the kind of cooperation that we see between Max and Jackie, and especially not a scam headed by the woman and dependent on her coolness, intelligence and resourcefulness.

In this he is strikingly like Jack Nicolet (Michael Keaton), the WPA cop who also thinks he is successfully controlling Jackie. Nicolet's mistake, according to Jackie, is to accept her explanation that Ordell's behaviour is based on fear of them: 'I got them [the cops] thinking Ordell's real nervous. They love thinking he's scared of them.' In much the same way Ordell is finally trapped and destroyed by his belief in Jackie's fear of him. Jackie is aware that this is Ordell's vulnerable point, instructing Max to tell him 'I've chickened out. I'm afraid of him. He'll like that,' and Ordell walks into the trap at the bail bond office because he wants to believe this explanation: 'You got her spooked.' This is played out in action in the fatal, crucial moment at the bond office, in which Ordell, entirely convinced by the reality of his image of a solitary, scared woman waiting for him, pushes past Max into the office and so presents himself as a target to be shot by the police.

Ordell is an example of a familiar American figure. He is a confidence man, 'a manipulator or contriver who creates an inner effect, an impression, an experience of confidence, that surpasses the grounds for it' (Lindberg, 1982). Again, such a figure invokes a host of American characters, from the gallery of individuals in Melville's *The Confidence Man* to Walter Neff or Charles Foster Kane. The fascination and the charm that American culture has often associated with the figure is present in Ordell, but in the particularly dark context of his inexorable decline.

Ordell relates most happily to objects or to figures whom he can treat as objects, and his con depends crucially on his domination of a specific linguistic and social area (that of the relations between black and white America) and the reading of an associated set of stereotypes and images. Tarantino marks his decline in terms of both control of language (compare his first and last conversations with Max) and place (compare Melanie's space with the junkie's). What is remarkable is not so much his moments of violence as those of passivity, as if he anticipates or intuits that once he steps outside the narrow set of terms that he can manipulate he will be subject to a level of violence that he cannot hope to contain. (Of course, we want in part to see this happen – I have not forgotten that Ordell is an arms dealer and a murderer.) But it remains an achievement of *Jackie Brown* that it presents its monster not just as the focus of a set of intersecting judgements and fantasies on the part of others: Jackie, Nicolet, Max. We see the world as Ordell sees it, as composed of disposable or consumable or actively degrading objects, human and otherwise. And we become aware, as he does not, that like a number of *noir* heroes before him, he is one such object, a part of this world, not protected from it.

3 Exploring the medium: film violence in *Reservoir Dogs* and *Pulp Fiction*

KING: Have you heard the argument? Is there no offence in't?
HAMLET (*of the players*): No, no, they do but jest, poison in jest, no
offence i' the world.

(*Hamlet*, Act III Scene II)

It comes as something of a shock to realise that the blinding of
Gloucester is primarily entertainment.

(Northrop Frye (1957), *Anatomy of Criticism*, p.94)

Introduction

Perhaps Tarantino, in a mood of wishing mildly to tease his questioners'
assumption of moral purpose, has done the significance and the nuance of
the violence deployed in his films a disservice through his relatively cool
and simple responses to questions about violence in movies and in his
movies. In analysing film violence it is important to be detailed and I want
to look closely at two occasions in the work, both of which have attracted
comment. The point of my analyses will be attempting to put them to work
to ask two, obviously related, questions. One is about how Tarantino uses
passages of violence to further his narrative, to make distinctions between
the various forms and meanings of violent behaviour that are open to
different figures and thus what paths his story can take. The other is to
interrogate the ways in which the presentation of film violence explores the
medium of film itself.

The writing on this subject seems frequently to proceed from the prem-
ise that 'graphic violence is an inescapable and ubiquitous characteristic
of contemporary cinema', as the opening sentence of *Screening Violence*
(Stephen Prince (ed.), 2000) states. Further, that as there are 'vast areas of
violence and bloodshed in our world' (Bosley Crowther, in Prince, op. cit.,

p.54) we now relate to screen violence as if violent acts are a commonplace part of life. '"Senseless" and "random" violence pervades our lives and is barely remarkable or specific any longer' (Vivian Sobchack, in Prince, op. cit., p.123). Certainly there are reports of violence and images of it – I would not wish to be thought to be suggesting that we experience elements of our world as other than fearsomely vicious. But there are three categories implicit here: (a) violence as we understand it on a cinema screen, as simulated, (b) violence as we understand it in, say, a news report, as edited but connected to actual pain and horror, and (c) violence as it appears in our presence, in, say, the car accident or the fight we see or participate in, unmediated by any form of screen. I am less worried by the tendency to collapse (a) and (b), but very concerned with the differences between these two and the third category, what we feel (or what we imagine we might feel) in the presence of violence.

Experiencing violence in the medium of film involves our awareness of the endlessly merciful operation of cinematic techniques. These techniques serve the need and the desire to rest for a moment in a viewed world, in which something so pervasive, and so threatening, as violence is made bearable. Editing is absolutely crucial here: somewhere at the core of our fear is time, the knowledge that at least in the cinema we will not have to look too closely, or for too long. The horror of watching (and the horror of the victim's knowledge of being watched) is happily not in our hands. Light is obviously important too: the control of the illumination of the image is part of another form of mercy, so that 'you don't see anything'. (The telling phrase is Richard Dyer's, in his discussion of 'Sight' in his analysis of David Fincher's *Seven* in the BFI Modern Classics series.) The contract between audience and film-makers is that the experience is one that is being, for better or worse, controlled. These techniques can become conventions that render even supposedly 'graphic' violence finally reassuring (it is what we expected to see) rather than in any way innovative or explorative of the medium. A contemporary example is *The Passion of the Christ* (Mel Gibson, 2004), an exercise in rendering on the cinema screen a version of the catholic imagery of the Passion, with its obviously famous art-historical sources. It is so massively controlled that while in one sense entirely graphic (watch the nails pierce the flesh) it is also entirely conventional (look at the editing of the shots of those same nails). Behind the way these images work lurks our fear that violence, were we to confront it directly, might have quite different qualities. This is not just a matter of actual danger to our own bodies, but to our perceptions. Would we have to look, in bright light, for longer than we could bear?

An act of violence can be thought of as unique, something that is happening to one or more specific bodies at the hands of one or more others, and is, or always threatens to be, irreversible, governed by laws from which there is no appeal, that actually are laws. But clearly this is not so simply true within the medium of film. A character killed in one part of a film can be seen again later on (as in *Pulp Fiction*), or the events of a film could be shown to us as proceeding from a violent event backwards (as in Gaspar Noé's *Irreversible* (2002)). One answer is that these are not contradictions of the laws but confirmations of them, occasions where we use them to understand and shape our reading of how time is being presented to us. But another voice argues that in film (not solely cartoons) there are not laws but choices. Bullets remarkably miss, or do not leave a mess; we can have as little or as much blood as we like. These choices depend on the uses that can be made of the techniques of the medium.

Violence and Narrative – Mr Blonde, the cop and the ear in *Reservoir Dogs*

There are arguably few more frequently quoted moments in Tarantino's work, or indeed moments in modern cinema invoked in discussions of the representation of violence, than the sequence of which one of the climaxes is the moment in *Reservoir Dogs* in which Mr Blonde cuts off the ear of the captive cop. The discussion of it tends to take it as an exemplary instance, to locate it as an outrageous example of something that is held to be a general trend. The strategy of such discussions is often to isolate a moment from the texture and narrative of the film surrounding it, so that nothing seems to lead up to or away from it, as if the violence made the rest of the film somehow disappear. You would rarely know at what point in the film a quoted scene occurs; it is as if moments of violence could be adequately accounted for outside the narratives in which they are embedded.

So I want to consider the context in the case of the ear-slicing, and associated torture, in *Reservoir Dogs*. It involves asking what we know, and do not know, about Mr Blonde, and how he does and does not resemble the other criminals in the film.

Thinking about this, the first thing we might note is that up to the point of the introduction of the captive cop the violence that we have seen is of two distinct kinds, both of which are different to what we shall see from this point onwards. The first of these offers violence as a form of play or physical knockabout, in which little or no permanent damage is done to the body. The second offers wounds that are much more radically destructive, but without showing us what has caused them, the acts that brought these effects about.

Play or knockabout violence is the note initially sounded through dumbshow: Blonde offering to 'shoot' White in the coffee-house sequence. It is also the mode of men on the ground physically fighting (Pink and Larry in the warehouse, Blonde and Eddie in Joe's office). In the former case this is out of an explosion of anger at each other, and in the latter in a kind of ritual of greeting. Both of these seem to have something to do with the world of the playground, a point specifically made in the dialogue in reference to the Pink/Larry fight.

The second form of violence, involving the graphic representation of its effects but not its causes, is shown in Orange's welter of blood; although this image is recurrent in the film so far, at this point we have not yet been taken back to the occasion of his receiving the gunshot. The only flashback to the immediate aftermath of the robbery has been treated in the style of a cops-and-robbers chase, with passers-by being knocked over but not shot. The most blatant example of this style is when Pink is hit by a car, but recovers within seconds without substantial injury. When he commandeers a car, he throws the female driver out of it without otherwise harming her. In the early conversation in the warehouse there have been references to graphically violent deaths, but what has been shown in flashback has not presented those deaths visually. We can sum this up by saying that what Tarantino has shown us at this point are either acts where no great harm is done, or harm that is disassociated from the act that caused it.

This takes us up to the moment in which Blonde announces to Larry and Pink that he has something to show them, and takes them outside to reveal the cop (Kirk Baltz) in the trunk of his car. What we then see (interrupted by the 'Mr Blonde' flashback, to which I shall return shortly) groups the three men together for a moment, but proceeds to make a distinction that involves putting Larry and Pink together, and placing them apart from Blonde.

It is Larry and Pink, not Blonde, who we see reaching into the trunk to grasp the cop, and it is these two who beat him up, first with kicks and then blows to the face. In this sequence, which is intercut against shots of Eddie talking on his mobile phone as he drives towards the warehouse, Blonde's presence is recorded through a shot in which he unwinds duct tape with which to bind the captive – the taping of the cop to the chair is not shown. By the time Eddie arrives Blonde has already taken up his 'back seat' position, perched on top of a shrouded car, where he will stay until the others leave and he descends to begin the torture of the cop.

The point of the organisation of what we are shown is to suggest that the cop has a completely different significance for Larry and Pink on the one hand, and for Blonde on the other. For Larry and Pink the cop is a captive who may be able to talk, to tell them who set them up, and a vent for their anger, frustration and fear at the situation they find themselves in. They have no other reaction to him: as a cop, he is not one of the 'real people' for them, and later they do not dispute Eddie's point that they will in due course kill him. (When the cop is executed, neither Larry nor Pink display any marked reaction.) We might question their interrogation as a strategy (thus agreeing with Eddie, who points out that whatever confession is beaten out of the cop will not necessarily be true) but understand it as an impulse, a desire to believe that their situation would be improved by being better understood. If it is not clear (to us, or to them) exactly how this might work, at least the idea of causality is apparent. They are enacting their violence for a reason to do with information and with revenge, which they could articulate if asked.

Blonde's violence represents something quite different, and two related lines help to establish this. One is his explanation of the shootings in the jewellery store: 'If they hadn't done what I told 'em not to, they'd still be alive today.' The other, a few moments later, occurs when Blonde is alone with the cop, who refers to Eddie as his 'boss'. Blonde replies: 'Excuse me, pal. One thing I want to make clear to you. I don't have a boss. Nobody tells me what to do.' (The speech is substantially expanded from the same point in the screenplay.) Blonde then slaps the cop's face, quite lightly, to accompany or emphasise the statement.

Clearly something about authority, and being controlled, is at issue. The third crucial piece of background is the flashback, which Tarantino places between the dragging of the cop out of the car and the beating in the warehouse. In the flashback we see Blonde arrive at Joe's office, where he is greeted as an old friend who has served Joe well. The scene dramatises the relations between Joe, Blonde and Eddie. What we see displayed is Blonde's feeling that he ought to be a key member of the crime family headed by Joe rather than the humble dependent, giving thanks for the food parcels he received in prison. This is implicit in Blonde's routine, abetted by Joe, in which he needles Eddie, claiming that he and Joe have been discussing Eddie's shortcomings. Eddie's calm removal of his watch and bracelet during this routine locates it as a ritual, a piece of performance concluded by the two men wrestling on the floor. Situating it in this way (and piling on details that emphasise the blend of aggression and familiarity between the younger men) suggest that these feelings are well known, an old story.

We could sum up the flashback sequence by reading it as expressing Blonde's desperate desire to belong, to be part of the family, to extend the role of the dutiful son to Joe that he has enacted for his four years in prison. We can place against it his lines about shooting the disobedient in the jewellery store, and not having a boss, as expressing an equally intense desire to disavow his subordination. (Although even after the disaster of the robbery, he continues in part to play the good son, waiting for Joe to turn up at the warehouse.)

Can the torture of the cop be explained by the unresolved paradox at the heart of this characterisation? I think it cannot, although the flashback expresses Blonde's knowledge of his isolation from all of the others. The torture is an act that takes place with Blonde effectively alone; although there are two other human beings in the space, both of them are present for Blonde only as things. He is indifferent to Freddy, perhaps assuming that he is dying. The cop is present for Blonde only as the provider of a physical sensation. This is, of course, not the viewer's position; although we are encouraged to forget about Freddy for a while, Tarantino's direction of the scene, his concentration on the cop's face, ensures that the cop is present as a human being for us.

What is radically evil about what we see is its purely visceral purpose, a desire to torture for the sensation it provides, existing as it might be in the same sensual world as the pleasure derived from a dance or a song (Blonde's little dance to the music here is important in expressing the connection, locating the torture as existing on this plane). So he wants to tie the cop up, to gag him, to castrate him, to burn him alive.

Tarantino (or Madsen?) gives Blonde two, I suggest related, and certainly repeated, gestures. One is that of violently throwing objects away (a drinks carton, a cigarette, the severed ear, the empty can of gasoline). The other is

Reservoir Dogs. Isolated from all others: Mr Blonde (Michael Madsen).
Source: British Film Institute.

a nervous response to dirt, or the idea of dirt, on his hands (fussing at them while sitting on the shrouded car, wiping them twice on the cop's shirt to remove gouts of blood). These gestures function at a level of meaning that is not specific (that is to say, I do not think the audience are asked to read them in an exact fashion) but is sufficiently pointed to be suggestive; although the actions are apart from the direct torture, they help us to read it. Even if there were not explicit clues such as the line immediately following the severing of the ear – 'Was that as good for me as it was for you?' – we would be able to connect the tortures to an increasingly intense marking of the release of orgasm, from expelling insignificant objects from oneself to the final climactic act, here represented as that of covering another with a strong liquid – 'That burn a little bit?' This is a climax that it is intended will be followed not just by the death but by the total dissolution of the other (in a mass of flame).

Whereas Blonde's torturing of the cop involves not seeing him as other than a function, or instrument (we might call it essentially pornographic), Blonde dies because he is equally inattentive to the suffering body of Freddy. This links Freddy and the cop but I think we cannot necessarily construct a reading of the actions here as a matter of a deliberate act of defence, or punishment. We see Blonde raising the lighter to torch the cop and the first bullets hit his chest: only then does Tarantino cut to Freddy. The first form of deadly ejaculation (the petrol, shortly to be followed by the flame) is answered by an equally visceral moment of discharge when Freddy unloads the entire magazine of his pistol into Blonde's chest.

The effect of Tarantino's decision not to show us Freddy until after he starts shooting (no shots of returning to consciousness, awareness of the torture, preparing to take action) presents the killing of Blonde not as a planned action but almost as a physical, automatic response. Later (when we are shown it) we shall connect this to the case of it that occurred in the robbery. Freddy's shooting of the woman driver of the getaway car is shown as a compulsive, apparently involuntary response to taking a bullet in the stomach. Both cases are marked by the gesture that expresses Freddy's shock, his attempt, after the action has overtaken him, to replay the gesture as if to capture it mentally. We see it here as Freddy raises the empty gun. It is as if the dumbshow of pointing it as if to fire again at Blonde can somehow retrieve his visceral action, can reclaim it by repetition as a willed, or thought through piece of behaviour.

To sum up: in trying to express how far this passage of violence furthers Tarantino's narrative, we might think of it as expressing something about how these different figures possess and control their violence. The violence of Pink and Larry is explicable, both to ourselves and to them. Blonde's 'amusement' with the cop, in contrast, possesses him rather than his controlling it, like the impulses towards dance or sexual excitement with which it is aligned. And its possession of him makes him fatally inattentive to the other person in the room.

The difficult case is Freddy. When we see Blonde die just at the point when he is about to burn the cop we are seeing something that, if we think about it, we want to see, something that ought to feel like an act of rescue, and a punishment of evil. But Freddy is not the avenging angel, ready with the one-liner, that Hollywood has given us (say, in some roles played by Clint Eastwood or Arnold Schwarzenegger). His impulse to kill is not established as an act of ratiocination/rescue/revenge, and our feeling about it, as the film continues, will be affected by the sight of two dead bodies – the cop, casually executed by Eddie a little later, and the woman in the car, shot without a moment's hesitation by Freddy.

Furthermore, there is the absence of words to make Freddy's acts interpretable. Here he says nothing. When he kills the woman in the car we see his lips move but no words emerge, as if he has no terms adequate to his own physical or moral death. The moments are opposites to the smart line that offers the executioner as a man (usually a man) of words, of speech. Tarantino returns violent death to speechlessness, to silence.

One of the most basic distinctions that Tarantino observes in terms of acts of violence is represented through speed: the difference between the blow or gunshot that neither perpetrator nor victim nor audience has time to anticipate, and the act involving deliberation or anticipation, again, possibly for perpetrator, victim, and audience. I have argued that the organisation of the first part of the film intends to split apart two sides of violence, the act and the bodily effect – most classically, say, the fired gun and the impact of the bullet. The point of this sequence is to connect them and then to look at their qualities. This reminds us that the connection can feel terrifyingly easy and direct (the wielded razor and the severed ear) can be comfortably achieved stuntwork (the blows and the bloodied cop) and can be deeply ambiguous (our view of Freddy as the saviour of the cop and the punisher of Blonde).

Another fine mess: clean and dirty violence in *Pulp Fiction*

The robbers in *Reservoir Dogs* are interested primarily in monetary gain; Blonde apart, most of them would have regarded a raid on the jewellery warehouse in which nobody was harmed as a complete success. As I noted in Chapter 1, violence is a tool of their trade, but it is not an essential ingredient of what they do. Possibly threat is such an ingredient, but the enactment of violence is not.

I want now to turn to another series of occasions of violence, but ones of a different kind, those associated with Jules and Vincent in *Pulp Fiction*. The enactment of violence is how Jules and Vincent earn a living; they kill people to Marcellus Wallace's orders. What we learn from their opening scenes in *Pulp Fiction* is not only this literal fact but a good deal about their attitude to it, which can be summed up as one in which they see what they do as inhabiting the realm of the ordinary, or the routine. This is the message of their introductory sequence in the car, with its chatter about cinemas in Holland and burgers in Paris – the note is one of relaxation, to establish that whatever it is this pair are driving towards, it holds nothing that they are especially concerned to anticipate. (We might contrast this with the coffee-house sequence in *Reservoir Dogs*, where the nervousness of figures such as Freddy or Pink is palpable.)

They enter an apartment building in which they have arranged a hit. The procedure, although it is not spelled out too deliberately, is that somebody has been planted in the apartment in question, and the plant will let them in at an exact, prearranged time. With the advantage of surprise they will then kill all the occupants of the apartment apart from the door-opener, and retrieve an item that belongs to Marcellus, a briefcase that contains something of striking value. (With a nod to Aldrich's *Kiss Me Deadly*, Tarantino denotes this by the glow that is thrown upwards when the case is opened, although there is no suggestion that, as in Aldrich's film, the contents of the case are dangerous.)

Entering the building the subject of their conversation becomes more apparently relevant to their assignment (in that it is about Marcellus and how he punishes people), but the treatment is almost abstract. As they walk towards their destination the discussion (the fate of Antwan Rocamorra and the implications of foot massage) is played as if they were a couple of Renaissance wits, using a consciously bawdy subject to score points and display knowledge.

What then follows, after the pair break off, 'get into character' and enter the apartment, is subject to some practical considerations. They cannot shoot the boys, Brett (Frank Whaley) and Roger (Burr Steers), right away, for they may not be able to retrieve the briefcase if it is not in the apartment. So they have to terrorise sufficiently to make them reveal the location of the case but not so much as to make them conceal it, realising that their position is hopeless. We can read Jules' discussion of hamburgers and the metric system (lifting the materials of the earlier conversation) as a calculated playing on the boys' fears, both ordinary and disconcerting, or rather disconcerting because it is so ordinary, the dialogue with Brett suddenly breaking off with the direct question concerning the case put to Roger. When Marvin (Phil Lamarr), who is the plant, the figure who opened the door, interrupts here, Jules shouts at him: 'I don't remember asking you a goddam thing' before returning the question to Roger. Why the shout? I suggest because Jules' system of interrogation is being interfered with. He did not know that Marvin could have supplied the crucial answer that renders all this unnecessary, and he wants, or needs, to obtain the information in his own way before killing the informants. It is noticeable that only a few seconds after Vincent has satisfied himself as to the contents of the case, Jules shoots Roger, and then works his way through the ritual of terrorising and then executing Brett.

It may be helpful to examine the contrast between what we see here and the sequence that I have just discussed, the torture of the cop by Blonde. We can sum up the difference by saying that Jules' treatment of the final few seconds of Brett's life has both a logical explanation (reducing the threat of any fight-back in Brett by terrorising him) and is also a working through of something premeditated, which expresses the fact that for him killing is a routine occasion. The memorised passage from Ezekiel that Jules declaims emphasises this, as it suggests that the words are not something learned for this occasion alone, but part of a performance that choreographs a killing. This is visually confirmed by Vincent's treatment of it as a signal, cocking his gun as Jules launches into Ezekiel. He has clearly heard this before. Comparing this with Blonde and the cop, we see an occasion of 'amusement' (to use Blonde's term) there as opposed to one of workmanship here, and the uniqueness of that evil pleasure as opposed to routine here. Another way in which the distinction can be expressed is that Blonde's behaviour is strongly associated with sexual excitement, while Jules' is equally clearly not so aligned.

It is expressive that at this time Tarantino gives us no shot of Brett's body – as soon as the job is done, he ceases to be present to Jules' or Vincent's consciousness. Something is about to happen that will disrupt Jules' sense of the routine nature of the occasion, but we do not see it yet, as Tarantino cuts to another panel of the story. When we return much later (in the panel titled 'The Bonnie Situation') it is to a reprise of the final moments leading to Brett's execution.

As we live through these seconds again there are changes made from the first sequence. Part of this is to do with the narrative; this time we are given another point of view, that of the 'fourth man', who was in the bathroom when Jules and Vincent entered the apartment, and who will shortly burst through the door and fire at the pair, strangely missing them with every shot, after which they execute him and leave. But there is other new material, visual rather than narrative. For the first time we see an image of the bullets hitting Brett, and the terrified collapse of Marvin on to the floor. His shocked mumbling at what he has just seen irritates Vincent – 'He's getting on my nerves' – and an exchange follows in which Jules has to tell Marvin, 'I'd knock that shit off if I were you.'

As this is not narratively necessary (and is interestingly not in the screenplay), why is it included? I suggest it underlines the massive difference in sensibility here between the hitmen, who have no reaction to the situation beyond a calculation of who is dead and who is not, and Marvin, to whom the violence is present as something awful and intimate happening to the body of another. Vincent is irritated because he is being presented with another way of seeing the world, by somebody who has been shocked by what they have just done. What is established is that there are apparently no terms in which either enacting violence, or seeing the effects of it, marks Jules and Vincent. Their composure seems unassailable, but all this is about to change.

As the three men drive away, and Vincent in conversation turns to address a question to Marvin in the back of the car, the latter is killed by a random discharge of Vincent's gun. The remaining two men, and the car, are covered in blood, an outpouring which is both profuse and exposing, not easily concealed. It is important that the effect is immediate, as if Marvin had physically ceased to exist in an instant, his body converted into this copious red mess. The effect of collapsing a longer passage in the screenplay here is to make the suddenness of the change much more marked.

The sense of panic and of vulnerability in Jules and Vincent, as if they were vampires suddenly exposed to the sunlight, is clearly a radical change not anticipated before this moment. The action is now as follows: the hitmen drive to the nearest safe house, that of Jules' friend Jimmie (Quentin Tarantino), and conceal the car in Jimmie's garage. They contact Marcellus, who in turn phones a fixer called the Wolf. The Wolf takes charge of the situation, and the passage ends when the car and its contents are safely disposed of at an auto-crushing plant. What is at issue becomes clearer here if we ask a literal question. Why do the two hitmen need further assistance? What needs to be done (clean the car, change clothing, drive the tidied car to a place where it can be quickly and finally disposed of) is all obvious and not in itself difficult. All that is needed is, say, the phone call to Marcellus in which they can be directed to the place for the disposal of the incriminating vehicle and body. Why do they need the services of the Wolf?

I suggest that Tarantino offers a way of reading the sequence that involves thinking about gendered modes of behaviour. We have seen that until this event, in everything from their banter to their actions in executing the boys, Jules and Vincent fit into familiar masculine stereotypes of calm, controlled power. The effect of the outpouring of Marvin's blood is to abolish the

Pulp Fiction. Loss of authority: the bloodied figures of Vincent (John Travolta) and Jules (Samuel L. Jackson) taking instructions from the Wolf. *Source*: British Film Institute.

assumption of masculine control, in part to feminise them. It is suggestive that the available safe house is one that Tarantino characterises as a domestic world in which gender roles are markedly reversed. The bread-winner is the absent Bonnie, while Jimmie is the one staying at home drinking gourmet coffee. The note is nicely expressed in Jimmie's shabby, rumpled dressing gown, a prop with a long history of expressing domestic-ity without power. The threat is the return, not of a male authority figure, but of Bonnie. In order to assume their role now, the stereotypically feminine one of cleaning up, the three men must be directed by a figure associated with a comic-book masculinity (the Wolf's name, his Porsche, his fast driving and his pride in it, his style of dress – and the casting, a nice joke, of Harvey Keitel in this role). Alongside the Wolf are the two other invocations of powerful masculinity: 'Monster' Joe, the owner of the car-disposal plant, whom we suggestively never see, and Marcellus at breakfast, at his most groomed in appearance and melodiously sonorous on the telephone to Jules. In both cases masculinity is underlined by the presence of the special woman, a kind of queen or princess: Mia, seen at her most composed in the sequence with Marcellus, and Raquel (Julia Sweeney), the princess of the wrecking business – 'Some day, all this will be hers' – who is the Wolf's girlfriend. It takes all this heavily underscored masculinity to wash away some blood.

Tarantino seems to want us to know that this sequence touches on matters that are both profound and familiar, as if he were retelling, or inventing, a fairy tale. There are some literal clues for us, a dialogue line about Beauty and the Beast, and this being a story with a monster and a wolf in it. We can think of it as a tale about blood, and the combination of repulsion and fear it induces, and again Tarantino makes some of the undercurrents of this subject explicit early on. It is in the scene in which Jules and Vincent wash their hands in Jimmie's bathroom. The business that culminates in Jules' line about Vincent's inefficient washing ('I used the same fuckin' soap you did, but when I finished the towel didn't look like no goddam maxipad') would be superfluous but for its invocation of menstrual blood. As evidence of the feminisation (and of fear of the feminine) evoked here we might recall that in fairy tale and elsewhere it is often women who are seen as unable to remove bloodstains (see, for example, Marina Warner's discussion of the Grimm Brothers' story of Fichter's Bird and the variations on the story of Bluebeard's castle in her *From the Beast to the Blonde*, 1994, pp.244–5, 255). Behind this detail, the distant background to the moment, is the whole mass of scholarly material that stresses the importance to the foundations of human culture of gendered attitudes to blood (see, for example, Chris Knight, 1991).

My point is that, however lightly and deftly invoked, these are images and subjects that do have a profound resonance for us. So Jules and Vincent, demasculinised by the blood, are restored to masculinity by the Wolf, or at least cleansed of blood and set back on the road to manhood (as the episode ends he calls them 'crazy kids').

The passage demonstrates both the range of Tarantino's uses of violence and his understanding of instability, the suddenness of the switch from control to the loss of it. The deaths of the boys in the apartment and the death of Marvin in the car could not be more sharply contrasted in terms of what a gunshot can be shown to do to a human body. As with my example from *Reservoir Dogs*, the subject is the two sides of violence, the act and the effect, and Tarantino seems to be setting up some connections and contrasts here.

We have seen a number of versions of what can happen when a gun is fired. They range from the bullet that does nothing, does not even touch its victim (the 'fourth man' shooting as he emerges from the bathroom) to the bullet that tidily switches a life off (Jules and Vincent shooting the boys) to the bullet that almost magically converts flesh into blood (Marvin's death). These variants are linked historically to cinematic modes of expressing death or escape from it. We are familiar with the lucky or miraculous escape as a trope that cinema offers us (closely related to its opposite, the scene in which every bullet eerily finds its exact mark). We can link the deaths of

Brett and Roger to the traditional gunplay of *noir* and the Western in classical Hollywood, full of rhetoric and lacking in blood, with its measured distance between killer and victim. Whereas the death of Marvin takes us to an extreme of the representation of death by gunshot in the post-Production-Code era of Hollywood film, where there can be more and more blood until through an act of metonymy death becomes simply blood, its horror represented on the screen by the explosion of a bag of red matter inside the car. The two questions that seem always to coexist for Tarantino are how kinds of violence operate within his dramatic worlds, and how they can be seen as cinematic techniques. Thus we are challenged to think about how we understand what we see, and how this relates to changing perceptions of what violence means to film audiences. I shall be taking up this subject in my discussion of *Kill Bill*.

4 Tarantino as screenwriter: *True Romance* and *Natural Born Killers*

In this chapter I want to look at two of Tarantino's early screenplays and consider what became of them on film, and what this can tell us. I am conscious of some of the difficulties of this exercise. One is the danger of treating the screenplays as if they represented the finished article on screen: as if, had Tarantino been given a chance to direct them, he would have filmed exactly this vision with no further change. Another concerns the exact status of the published screenplays themselves, which is not entirely clear. Probably all that we can say is that they represent what Tarantino is happy to put his name to as representing points of departure, the texts frozen at the stage at which they passed from his hands into those of the directors and producers of the films. This is at any rate the assumption that I am making in what follows.

True Romance

True Romance presents a number of points of interest. As Tarantino's first major screenplay, we can look to it for scenes that are particularly suggestive or resonant in the light of his later work as a director. I suggest that there are two of these, the scene involving Cocotti (Christopher Walken) and the death of Cliff (Dennis Hopper), and the extended hotel-room scene between Alabama (Patricia Arquette) and Virgil (James Gandolfini) that ends with Virgil's death. Both scenes are extended episodes of violence built largely or entirely around two figures, one of whom has little or no role elsewhere in the film.

There are also two respects in which the screenplay and film diverge that are substantial enough to bear discussion. One is the structural issue of the order in which the elements of the narrative unfold, particularly the first half of the film, and the other is the matter of the survival of the couple, that is, specifically the survival of Clarence (Christian Slater). (There are of course many other smaller characteristic moments that could be discussed. It seems almost redundant to say that we can observe in the screenplay, and carried on into the films, a number of examples of the kind of small felicities of writing of which Tarantino's work is full.) I shall return to these topics, but before looking at them in detail I think it will be helpful to say something about the kind of narrative that *True Romance* is and, perhaps as significantly, the paths it chooses not to pursue.

The nature of this romance can be defined by looking at the very end of the narrative, where Clarence is explaining himself and Alabama to the rich Lee (Saul Rubinek): 'Me and my wife are minimum-wage kids, two hundred thousand [dollars] is the world.' This is perhaps the only direct expression of something that is very persistently implied, that Clarence and Alabama are a couple whose romance is based not on difference but on similarity, a recognition of themselves in each other. (No trace of the plot of the call girl and the millionaire (*Pretty Woman*), or the businessman and the secretary (*Working Girl*) here.) We never see them quarrel; their one brief difference, immediately after the death of Drexl (Gary Oldman), is simply based on a misconception by one of what the other meant. Thus what they have to address is not the qualities that distance themselves from each other, but rather their mutual sense of disinheritance, their relation to the world that is controlled by the powerful. For them good fortune is

True Romance. Clarence (Christian Slater) and Alabama (Patricia Arquette): 'Me and my wife are minimum-wage kids, two hundred thousand [dollars] is the world.' *Source*: British Film Institute.

experienced as a kind of illusion, their world a context in which they are always actual or potential victims.

So the plot of *True Romance* can be characterised as a series of episodes in which an attractive and well-suited pair of young lovers find each other (which is to say, find some stages or settings in which they can approach each other) but where these places are anomalies in a larger world that can be described only as a chaos of individual selfishness. They cannot flee that world – they can only attempt, nervously and marginally, to manipulate it. This results in a journey towards a point at which the illusion of order, or at least of an orderly jostling between power groups, disintegrates into a maelstrom of violence. According to whether we are looking at the screenplay or the released film of *True Romance*, this violence either destroys them or they miraculously escape from it.

Tarantino constructs his plot around a MacGuffin (Hitchcock's term, coined by Angus MacPhail, for a device that motivates action in plotting a movie) in the form of the contents of a suitcase that Clarence acquires by a fluke. The case contains something of sufficient value to be capable of changing Clarence and Alabama's world entirely, and so it cannot be ignored or rejected – a large quantity of uncut cocaine. It is valuable but also deadly, both in the local sense that it is a drug, capable of negative effects on the lives of its eventual consumers, and in the less direct sense that it acts as a magnet for the hoods trying to retrieve it and the cops anxious to make a bust.

The idea of a man who acquires a possession that is both a treasure trove and a source of potential disaster can be traced back to a number of earlier films. Tarantino has spoken of his liking for *Nightfall* (Jacques Tourneur, 1956), in which the package that the hero acquires by chance is the proceeds of a heist, and he makes direct allusion in *Pulp Fiction* to *Kiss Me Deadly* (Robert Aldrich, 1955) in which the image of uncontainable energies is attached directly to the object in the briefcase, an unstable material that explodes as the film concludes. I suggest that behind these variants is the representation of the final instability of a concentration of a large amount of power/energy/money into a small space. Eventually a reaction takes place that cannot be reversed: either the package finally explodes of its own accord (*Kiss Me Deadly*) or, acted on by the forces surrounding it, it is ruptured so that it distributes its contents into the world again (as in the cocaine exploding as the gunfire hits the bag in the hotel room in *True Romance*, or the stolen banknotes bursting out of the suitcase in Kubrick's *The Killing*).

A variation of this plot is offered in *True Romance*. As the cocaine explodes and most of the cast in the hotel room die in the shootout, Alabama picks up another case, the one containing the $200,000 that was payment for the cocaine, and makes her escape. This is represented by Tarantino (and by Tony Scott) as not so much an act of careful deliberation or coolness under fire as an impulse or a fluke, almost like Clarence's getting the cocaine in the first place. Perhaps the point being made is that who lives and dies here is not a matter of moral judgement (hardly), but more a matter of the series of chances, ones that reflect a random pattern of loss and gain, life and death. (I shall come back to this when we look at the differences between the death lists in Tarantino's and Scott's versions of the ending.)

It is important to look at one subject that the screenplay of *True Romance* scrupulously avoids, that of revenge. There are two large opportunities for it. Tarantino has pointed out (see the section titled 'Omission' in the preface to the *True Romance* screenplay) that Alabama could die in her fight with Virgil, and 'it would give Clarence something to do for the last fifteen minutes – avenge her', but this does not happen. It is Virgil who dies, and he is not a subject for revenge. Another remarkable decision is that one of the most striking scenes in the narrative, the torture and execution of Cliff (Clarence's father) by Coccotti, has no consequences. There is no evidence that Clarence ever knows about it, or wonders how the hoods caught up with him. Thus in Tarantino's screenplay there is no trace of a revenge motive at any point – nobody kills or is killed as a consequence of an earlier act, or as the follow-up to a previous contact. Rather, the persistent configuration is the scene of extreme violence between characters who have never met before: Coccotti and Cliff, Clarence and Drexl, Alabama and Virgil (the order in the screenplay). A related point is made by omitting Coccotti from the hotel shoot-out. Assuming that the current plotting (that Clarence did not know that this man killed his father) was retained, if Coccotti were reintroduced here and were to die in the gunfire, we, at least, would be avenged for what we saw him do to Cliff. Tarantino avoids these plots: there is to be no getting even here, and therefore none of the sense of a restored order or of an act that brings relief, that might have been present. Rather, the mode is of a romance disposed against the background of a world in which the only governing principle is the exercise of power, the dominant mood the belief in the ability to use violence to injure or destroy.

The connecting thread between the three violent encounters that I have mentioned is that in each case one party (Coccotti, Drexl, Virgil) begins the scene convinced of their dominance, sure that in this kind of world the winner is always the man with the most armaments, and with the least conscience about using them. They are men who see the exercise of violence as a dramatic ritual that is in their possession, and construct their victims as simply terrorised or passively resigned, dominated not only by the firepower of the opponent but by his experience, by the knowledge that killing (or ordering a killing) is nothing to him. This is in itself not unusual, and the drama of such a sequence is easily available. It is the possibility of a reversal that happens by a lucky chance, a second of distraction on the part of the would-be killer, or some piece of knowledge that he lacks, or an intervention by another figure. This is the case in the most conventional of the three encounters – Drexl dies because his attention momentarily lapses and allows Clarence space to pull a gun.

In the other two cases, what enters into the equation and affects the relation between the principals is their possession and understanding of the world of sexuality. In both cases the subject is present before the reversal. It is implicit in Coccotti's speech on lying and its pedantically exact assertion of knowledge of women and their pantomimes of mendacity. Cliff's reply (his speech about the ancestry of Sicilians with its crafted combination of racial and sexual insult) has its intended effect of demolishing Coccotti's command of the violence he possesses, so that what was planned by Coccotti to be a torturing interrogation becomes an instant execution. At least, this is the case in Tarantino's screenplay, another instance of his interest in the movement between deliberate and spontaneous violence. In the film, the added exchanges between the two characters slightly blur the sense of Coccotti's unnerved switch from complete control to its opposite.

In the scene between Alabama and Virgil the drama is more extended, but the terms are not dissimilar. Again, the speeches from Virgil indicate his control of violence (explaining how killing has become easier and easier for him). Virgil also believes he controls the sexual dimension of the scene, beating up Alabama while counterpointing the violence with comments on her looks. But sexual feeling is what crucially escapes his control when he tears open his shirt and offers her (it seems clearly a piece of sexual teasing) a stab at his chest. Her rejection of the sexualised stab at the heart or groin for the strategic target of the foot destroys this sexual confidence, and is the first move in the series of smashes and grabs that are governed not by his command of the situation but by the chances that come the way of the two fighters. I do not think we are meant to see the reversal as a simple one in Alabama's favour, but rather an opportunity to use her luck and resource-fulness. In this she is conceived much in the manner of the 'final girl' who, as Carol Clover has pointed out, frequently defeats the male predator in horror films.

In terms of dialogue and the detail of action there are a few small changes that take place between the ways these sequences appear in the screenplay and their renditions in the film, and these seem mostly insignificant (such as the cutting of part of Drexl's speech in which he proposes to abuse Alabama sexually (see the screenplay, p.66), possibly a matter of not wanting the crudeness of the reference to interrupt the flow of the scene).

The important changes seem to be more matters of style. Scott extends the time that is taken over certain actions, so that the enactment of two crucial pieces of violence (Coccotti's execution of Cliff, and Virgil's first striking of Alabama) are played with spaces in which an audience can anticipate the horror to come, rather than the shock of the sudden. The death of Marvin in *Pulp Fiction* (see my discussion on p.48) would be a good example of the latter mode in Tarantino's direction, where the opposite movement occurs: an extended scene in the screenplay is shrunk into a single moment on film. We might further define this difference by saying that Scott is sometimes concerned with the possibility of a sequence of violence generating a moment to enjoy a striking visual image, as objects are smashed up. The shot in which Clarence hurls Drexl into a bank of fish tanks (which is not in the screenplay) produces such an image as the tanks shatter.

Another of Scott's strategies is to present a whole sequence in terms of the visual imagery of menace – for example, smoke and a palette of dark-blue tones in the scene with Coccotti and Cliff. Tarantino is perhaps both less concerned with playing with familiar images of evil – he has spoken of his dislike of smoke – and, in the screenplay, less concerned with the staging of violence, as presented through the smashing up of objects.

My final topic is that of the structural changes that take place between screenplay and film. I shall begin by annotating the shift in the location of the episodes of Clarence and Alabama's romance. The broad distinction is that in the screenplay Tarantino concentrates in the opening sequences on Cliff: his encounter with the young couple that is Alabama and Clarence, their departure and then his death at the hands of Coccotti. After these episodes the film moves to LA, and the story of Alabama and Clarence's romance, through to the death of Drexl, is all told in flashback as an implicit answer to Dick (Michael Rapaport) addressing the question of what love is like. Scott dismantles this timescheme, effectively putting the film into chronological order, so that the Clarence/Alabama romance sequences begin the film, and only after they are complete (from first meeting to marriage) is the figure of Drexl introduced and shortly afterwards killed by Clarence. This is followed by the scenes with Cliff.

The effect of the changes seems to be not all that difficult to estimate. In Tarantino's order of events, in which Cliff's sequences open the narrative, our attention is more equally distributed between the three figures of father, son and daughter-in-law (in that we are not yet privy to the story of the couple's romance). The death of Cliff, although shocking, makes the point that this event is part of a world in which such violence is endemic. The scenes with Cliff/Clarence/Alabama are sandwiched between two death scenes. The later one is Cliff's execution, and the earlier is the execution of two other drug dealers by Drexl. This is Tarantino's second sequence in the screenplay, and one in which Drexl shoots everybody else in the room, 'surveys the carnage, spits, and walks out'. This is crucial in establishing a mood that is confirmed by Cliff's death. When the romance scenes follow they are played, as it were, as memories screened against this background of carnage.

The first deaths to occur in Scott's film are also of the drug dealers, but this sequence now occurs later in the film and the background for it is now the romance sequences that have preceded it. (It is also notable that Scott does not have Drexl kill all the other figures: the sequence seems to function more simply as a way of setting him up as an unsympathetic figure.)

The difference might be thought of as between a vision in which these sequences are essentially intended to characterise the irredeemable violence of the world (Tarantino) and one in which they are used to propose some degree of causality (Scott). For Tarantino, when the drug dealers and Cliff die, it is because that is the kind of environment he is describing. Further, when Drexl dies (much later in the screenplay) at Clarence's hands, it is because Clarence is a part of that world too, not separate from it.

For Scott, when the drug dealers die it is so that we see how dangerous and evil Drexl is, and we go directly into the sequence in which Clarence kills him. (Drexl's treatment of the drug dealers is more clearly linked with his abuse of Alabama, and there is a stronger sense of revenge on Clarence's part when he kills Drexl.) When Cliff dies (much later in the film) it is shocking but logical, as the film has already established the romantic couple, and Cliff's act can be seen, more obviously than in Tarantino's version, as an act of noble sacrifice by the older generation.

We can relate these different approaches to Scott's decision to allow Clarence to survive the shoot-out, and the happy ending with the couple and their child on the beach that follows this in the film. In the screenplay Clarence dies, and the narrative ends with Alabama alone with the case of money. (According to Jami Bernard (1995, p.87), a version of the happier ending was first written by Roger Avary at an early stage in pre-production.) Tarantino objected to the change, on the grounds that 'my ending has a symmetry with the whole piece' (preface to the screenplay), and Scott agreed to shoot an alternative ending along the lines of the screenplay, but released the film with the version in which Clarence lives. The deleted sequence is available on the most recent DVD release.

Consider the full list of those who survive in each version. In Tarantino's ending, it is Boris (Eric Allan Kramer), Alabama and Dick. They are respectively a wounded veteran from the front line, the scene's single woman (unarmed for most of the sequence), and the entirely unarmed man that nobody has paid any attention to. This seems to imply that in a final shoot-out of this kind, there is no secure logic to who lives and who dies, only an argument that those perceived as doing the shooting are themselves more likely to be shot at.

In Scott's film, Clarence lives, Boris dies along with his comrades, and Alabama and Dick survive in much the same terms (though Scott does not use the gag in the screenplay about other worlds indifferent to this one, where Dick takes refuge in another hotel room where some girls are so absorbed in working out that they do not notice him or the mayhem around them). Clarence's survival is clearly the anomaly: he is armed, he is a principal player in this business. One could defend it by suggesting that the element of random chance here could render any survival plausible. It does generate one effective image, that of Clarence and Alabama staggering through the hotel car park as the cops arrive, just a couple of minimum-wage kids that nobody notices.

I suggest that the issue of the ending relates to the divergence between Tarantino and Scott that I have discussed. For Scott, the element of successful vengeance against the kinds of monsters that are represented in Drexl and Virgil is much more emphatic. The idea is that the vengeance is the more complete in that we triumph in seeing that the couple who struck those monsters down are poised and happy in the final shots. For Tarantino, with his love of the films, and the plots, of a director such as Jean-Pierre Melville, the rules are more like those of a game of chance, in which an individual's luck will simply run out, as it was bound to, sooner or later.

Natural Born Killers – violence without regeneration

Natural Born Killers was Tarantino's second completed major screenplay, his second attempt, as he puts it, at something 'written to be my first film'. The contested history of the treatment of the script and the production of Oliver Stone's film has been discussed at length (see Further Reading) and I shall not repeat it here. It is sufficient to note that the difficulties and the substantial rewriting of the script led Tarantino to take only 'story by' credit when the film was released. My approach will be first to consider Tarantino's published screenplay, beginning by looking at some of the ways in which it departs from, and connects with, the themes and problems of *True Romance*, and attempting to give a reading of it in this form. I shall then go on to a discussion of Stone's film and some of the ways in which the material was changed.

The *Natural Born Killers* screenplay

True Romance, as filmed, clearly references Terrence Malick's *Badlands* in its use of the same Erik Satie music, and in Alabama's opening voice-over. If we ask what aspect of Malick's film is being evoked, then the answer is perhaps that what the films have in common is a quality of strangeness, or perceived lack – the eeriness of Satie's music played over images of a melancholy landscape, and a voice that speaks touchingly of a memory and that does not lay claim to more than a limited understanding of what we are about to see, more limited chorus than narrator. In *Badlands*, of course, this melancholy is connected to the evocation of a lost past, the America of the early 1950s, and in *True Romance* to another traditional area of American imagery, the decaying industrial city.

In the *Natural Born Killers* screenplay there is another form of connection we can make to *Badlands*, this time not to atmosphere but to narrative. The background story of Mickey and Mallory is told in small flashbacks, just after the credit sequence, and it is as follows. A young couple are in conflict with the girl's parents who are hostile to their relationship. The boy appears to have no parents, or they are hardly mentioned. The couple murder the girl's parents, set fire to the house as they flee, and travel through a series of American locations, committing further murders until eventually apprehended by the police.

With the exception of the brief presence of the girl's mother, this is closely analogous to the outline plot of *Badlands*. The connection is unsurprising, in a way – both are versions of an American story of lighting out on your own, of the death of a father being a central element of a narrative in which you take up with a companion and set out across America, of which, of course, Mark Twain's *The Adventures of Huckleberry Finn* remains the most distinguished example. *Badlands* and the *Natural Born Killers* screenplay represent the negative version of this myth. By killing the father, the child (or children) attains a kind of freedom or release but their voyage cannot be one of exploration or enlightenment. It becomes only an opportunity to repeat acts of violence until finally killed or captured.

I see the difference between Tarantino's first two screenplays as follows. *True Romance* is about the odds for and against success for a young couple who exist in a world of ubiquitous violence (or, we might simply say, exist in America). In Tarantino's view, they are not very good odds – in Tony Scott's a little better. *Natural Born Killers* is something much closer to a satire, a meditation on what an ideal couple might look like in a culture in which energy is strongly identified with violence (again, we could just call this America, but Tarantino includes a brief nod to global media culture).

Kit (Martin Sheen) and Holly (Sissy Spacek) in *Badlands* are at sea in the world – Malick seems continually to offer us the images of a culture slightly beyond the reach of their imaginations or understanding. They represent violence attached to a sense of puzzlement. Mickey and Mallory are the opposite of them, and to Clarence and Alabama in *True Romance*, in lacking any sense of being odd or anomalous. The nature of their violence is expressed most succinctly through the selection of their victims. Tarantino uses his opening pre-credit sequence to stress that they kill simply what is nearest to them. They do not seek out the three rednecks who arrive at the coffee shop and whom they murder. The choice of the final victim in this scene is a piece of business in which Mallory's 'eenie, meanie, minie, mo' rhyme is exactly what it seems, not a form of teasing but simply an indication that it does not matter to them who lives and who dies. There is no suggestion, here or elsewhere in the screenplay, that Mickey and Mallory are significantly motivated in their killing by greed for money, or by racial or class hatred, or by sexual excitement, or by revenge. (There is one local exception to this, the killing of Scagnetti by Mallory, which is a deliberate response to his torture of her earlier.) We find that their tale develops into one of the most American of stories, a rescue narrative, but there is no sense that their escape from prison at the end of the screenplay is an escape to anywhere, that they have an idea of a world in which they would be free. They differ from some of Tarantino's earlier and later perpetrators of violence in that they are not doing a job of which violence is the whole or a part, as is the case, say, for Coccotti and Virgil in *True Romance*, or all of the main characters in *Reservoir Dogs*.

A way of expressing this is to think of Mickey as a kind of end point of a tradition of representation of the American hero figure. He is no longer the hunter, with the complex mythic relation to the hunted creature and thus to nature that runs through so many classic American works of art. (I think it possible that Tarantino, in using the pre-credits coffee-shop sequence to emphasise Mickey's skills, that he is equally fast and deadly with a knife and a gun, invites us both to make this connection and to appreciate this difference.) His violence has no larger function with respect to the family or sexuality, neither one of defence nor destruction. He has only one emotion, his feeling for Mallory, but that is strikingly confined to, or satisfied by, his image of them kissing, as if this is as far as his imagination is able to take him. His effect on those with whom he comes in contact is as random as if he were the carrier of a deadly disease. We could say, he is the American hero with everything but the violence left out.

If this represents a development from the traditional figure of the American hero, then what of the heroine? Mallory's opening word in the screenplay is 'Nada' (nothing), and the note that Tarantino strongly emphasises in the screenplay is her wordlessness. Apart from the flashback to her speech to the female psychiatrist, which is devoted to the worthlessness of explanation and punishment, she does not speak while in jail, but sings or chants. She has almost no significant lines until reunited with Mickey in the final part of the narrative, and even at this point has little to convey apart from her admiration for him. Her violence is evidently a substitute for language. Again this is firmly established in the pre-credit sequence, by her wordless beating to death of Otis, one of the rednecks in the coffee shop. It is emphasised again towards the end, where Scagnetti's verbal sexual abuse is answered not with words but with escalating violent action: she spits in his face, breaks his nose, tries to break his back. Although she does use conventional firearms elsewhere, her most striking passages of violence seem to be when her instrument of aggression is her own body, even when she uses it ineffectively: for example, in knocking herself out by charging the cell door.

This extreme and energetic violence (directed almost invariably towards men) seems to be linked with a sexual imagination that is almost undeveloped. Mallory also refers to herself and Mickey mostly in a way that goes no further than an embrace, and at the very end of the screenplay she can still talk about how they can now 'enjoy each other's company', and is worried about having used the word 'fucking' on air. Thus the extreme ease and practice and fluency of the couple's violence goes along with a limited range of expression in the realm of the sexual. They are not, in the traditional sense that horror movie monsters or psychopaths often are, punishers of sexual activity, and their violence is not read by their world as an expression of repressed sexuality. Rather they are aware of their sexuality (for example, Mallory's sense of the response to her erotic body, Mickey's sense of the fixed attention when he tells a dirty joke), but only as something that is functional in the exercise of their violence.

Thus they are a kind of satirical ideal couple: a combination of wildly colourful violence with undeveloped sexual expression, thought of as 'devotion' or 'romance'. Here lies, for a population reconciled to violence but with a deeply problematic view of sexual activity, the root of the couple's popularity.

What of the other figures? There is little of the ordinary world in the screenplay: we might say that as soon as that world wanders into the scene it is set upon and destroyed by Mickey and Mallory. Rather, there is a standard subject of satire: what Northrop Frye terms the rapacious or incompetent professional (see, for example, *Anatomy of Criticism*, p.309). This is the group for whom figures like Mickey and Mallory are raw material, a dangerous but valuable resource that can be used to produce a bestseller (Scagnetti), or a television show (Wayne, the 'commando journalist') or a feature film (Neil Pope). The narrative shows that when Mickey and Mallory directly come into contact with this world they destroy it too (only Pope, who never meets the couple but simply embroiders their story, escapes harm). Mallory kills Scagnetti, and the screenplay ends with Wayne being shot to death by the couple. The figures treated most positively (and allowed the most uncomplicated comedic presence) are simply those at the greatest distance from the presence of the couple's violence. An example is Buffy St McQueen, the actress who plays Mallory in *Thrill Killers*, the film based on the couple's exploits, and who sounds in her one long speech strikingly like Tarantino in interview. Thus there is no contrast between good and bad worlds here. The group around Wayne does not represent the 'good family' as opposed to the 'bad couple'. They are rather a group blind to everything apart from their assigned tasks, and in the case of Wayne's assistant, 'Unruly Julie', totally without speech (it is at one point stated that Julie was born without a tongue). Wayne and Julie present a loosely parallel couple to Mickey and the self-silenced Mallory, but not a positive version of them.

We might conclude and sum up by saying that in the screenplay Tarantino is looking at a culture in which a heterosexual couple who can claim to be young, physically attractive and 'devoted' are capable of being admired no matter what. This is especially so if they conform to an idea of the couple where power – especially the power denoted by the ability to use language to mesmerise, compel, negotiate – is held by the man. The inclusion of Unruly Julie and her muteness is highly suggestive in this context, presumably intended by Tarantino to support the subject of the silencing of the female voice made in his writing of the Mallory part.

A substantial shift between the screenplays of *True Romance* and *Natural Born Killers* is that the emphasis on the woman's imagination in the former disappears in the latter. The satirical point is that the loss of that 'dazzling imagination' is one part of what makes Mickey and Mallory such acceptable heroes to the mass.

Oliver Stone's *Natural Born Killers*

It does not seem appropriate, in a book on Tarantino, to mount a full-scale analysis of Stone's film. Equally, it is difficult to be silent about it, as it seems so deeply unsuccessful. It has the asset of a group of highly effective (and appropriately cast) players, and some single images of striking beauty. What most overtly damages it is its style, an ineffective use of techniques, which include black-and-white photography, skewed camera angles, and various form of back-projection. These techniques are used so incoherently and so pervasively that they are unreadable other than for their assertion that the film cannot allow itself to hesitate, to appear for a moment irresolute about what it thinks it is doing, or we are making of it. The result is that techniques become meaningless gestures, giving the film a quality of restlessness and desperation that may reflect a lack of faith in the script as finally written and performed.

What I want to consider, largely for what light they may throw on what Tarantino does not choose to do, or is not interested in, are some of the ways in which Stone and his scriptwriters changed the shape and emphases of the original screenplay. There seem to be three major areas of change, which are not easy to disentangle from each other: narrative structure, the desire to give an explanation for behaviour, and sexual activity.

The change in narrative structure is in part a matter of putting events back into chronological order, not unlike the changes I discussed earlier in Scott's film of *True Romance*. While the pre-credit coffee-shop sequence is retained, the film proceeds into an extended account, one that is more or less chronological, of the tale of Mickey (Woody Harrelson) and Mallory (Juliette Lewis) – their meeting, their killing of Mallory's parents, their wedding, and their journey across America, killing as they go. Only after their capture, in the later part of the film, does the narrative return more or less to Tarantino's structure.

Why does this matter? It matters partly because it raises a question of our perspective on the couple. Tarantino, taking Mickey and Mallory almost entirely after their capture, offers their story as a matter of report, something that we can only have access to as a brief flashback (as in the single shot in the screenplay recounting the killing of Mallory's father and the two shots that cover the murder of her mother). Otherwise it is mediated through the codes of popular culture, in the footage from Wayne's *American Maniacs* TV programme, or the *Thrill Killers* footage. The point made in the screenplay is that in the tales being told by McClusky to Scagnetti and by Wayne and his crew, we are seeing something that is already legend being recounted. (In *Thrill Killers* we find that the legend is already up for a little rewriting.) What is not possible is any unmediated access to the past, nor – and this is an important note – is there any desire for it.

Dismantling this structure takes away the sense of the remoteness of the past of Mickey and Mallory. Stone replaces it with a series of sequences that, however hysterical stylistically, claim to give an account of the couple's past that explains their murderous behaviour. Tarantino's position, that we do not and cannot know why Mickey and Mallory are as they are, and that perhaps the culture that feeds on them is not interested in knowing, is replaced by a less radical and more comforting narrative through which we can apportion blame. The initial example is the clearest: the information that Mallory has been sexually abused by her father.

What Stone argues amounts to saying that these adult murderers are the product specifically of dysfunctional or abusive families, the explanation given variously for the behaviour of Mallory, Mickey and Scagnetti (Tom Sizemore), who also kills a young woman in the course of the film. The effect of such an explanation is to some extent to excuse them, to offer them as victims of their specific traumas (their bad families) rather than the more uncomfortable thought that they are a logical product of the larger culture that nurtured them, and us.

Having identified sexuality as the villain of the piece, of course it plays a dominant part in the presentation of the couple and their relation to each other in the rest of the film. It is presented both negatively (Mallory's sexual insecurity and aggression, Mickey's routine terrorising of a captive woman in a motel) and positively (the wedding sequence). The careful distinction between the couple's relation to sex and their relation to violence that is important to Tarantino's screenplay is completely abandoned, replaced by a vision in which almost all sexual activity inevitably collapses into violence of some kind. An example of the change is the scene between Scagnetti and Mallory in her cell, in which he taunts her sexually. Played in the screenplay as a scene in which Scagnetti's salaciousness meets, suddenly and shockingly, wordless and extreme violence from Mallory, in the film it becomes a predictable slide from seduction to mutual violence as both characters compulsively repeat their pasts.

It is unsurprising that these changes render some of Tarantino's more suggestive ideas inoperable in the film. The reordering of the narrative removes any sense of Mallory's silence, and the figure of Unruly Julie effectively disappears. There is a woman producer who is associated with Wayne (Robert Downey Jr), but she is given only routine material. And Stone drops everything involving *Thrill Killers*, with its engaging, affectionate view of how Hollywood serves up its Movie Mickey and Movie Mallory.

It can perhaps be argued that there is little point in anatomising these changes, but I suggest that it does present very clearly some elements of Tarantino's thinking. He understands very clearly how sex and violence can be connected but also how they can be separated, and he dislikes an insistence on easy explanation. In the lost film that is represented in the screenplay of *Natural Born Killers*, he asks us to bear with a story that won't tell, at least not in any literal, vulgar way.

5 Landscapes

Los Angeles is the world capital of the detached private house.

(W.A. McClung (2000), *Landscapes of Desire: Anglo mythologies of Los Angeles*)

Introduction

In this chapter I want to reflect on the settings of the films and how we are directed to see them: how places and spaces relate to their narratives and subjects. Tarantino's presentation of the urban landscape might not be thought to be a particularly interesting aspect of his work. He is not interested in an area's famous landmarks, or in presenting a panoramic view of a city. In terms of settings he rarely draws attention to the spectacular in the first three films, and often seems more interested in presenting generic rather than highly individual settings. Most of his characters are shown as inhabiting places that are familiar to them, or treating an unfamiliar setting as if it does not much surprise them. (Vincent's reaction to Jack Rabbit Slim's in *Pulp Fiction* would be an example of the latter.) But Tarantino's interest in how these settings weigh on his characters' and his audience's attention, and what actions they enable and what is prohibited in them, is nonetheless an important part of the films.

Some spaces, and thus their meanings, reveal themselves to us quite gradually or partially. Establishing shots are at points markedly absent, and where Tarantino does use them, he seems to enjoy making them overt, marked either by being shots that include signs (the 'Hawthorne Grill' in *Pulp Fiction*) or by using subtitles to announce them ('Del Amo Mall/ Torrance, California/Largest indoor Mall in the World' in *Jackie Brown*).

If there is a single aspect of place that is important to Tarantino's characters, it is the various kinds of differences between exteriors and interiors. It would be possible to argue that the exploration of a range of feeling and experience related to this, from absolute exposure to apparently complete privacy, constitutes a prominent characteristic of Tarantino's work in the first three films.

One space that connects the films can be considered here. It is a crucial mediation between interior and exterior in modern experience: the inside of a moving car, offering the chance to allow the outside world to pass at a distance, and sometimes to flee from the threat posed by it. Something that perhaps makes it attractive to Tarantino is that it is not possible to photograph the inside of a car, or really to see it, as a whole. It is an entirely familiar kind of space, a tight interior of a special kind of awkwardness, where seated figures cannot all look directly at each other easily or for long (contrasting, for example, with a table in a café, which offers exactly that possibility).

So Tarantino shows us that a moving car can be a good place for conversation and anecdote among acquaintances (the four thieves discussing Pam Grier in *Reservoir Dogs*, Jules and Vincent's conversation about food in *Pulp Fiction*, Jackie and Max's first scene together in *Jackie Brown*). But each film also shows us a character's death in a vehicle: Mr Brown in *Reservoir Dogs*, Marvin in *Pulp Fiction*, Beaumont and later Louis in *Jackie Brown*. None of these are the logical consequence of the technology of speed itself. That is, none are the result of car crashes; all of them are unexpected and shocking.

Perhaps Tarantino is relying on something that we know, or feel, about this particular generic space – that its familiarity, almost its homeliness, is what makes us feel content in it, but that in a matter of seconds it can be converted into a horror, a place of blood and death. There is deep uneasiness here, a question of helplessness, and of the potential denial of significance of place, a feeling that we should not die in the same place as we have casual conversations. Perhaps Tarantino, in his consistent presentation of both sides of this coin, wants to ask us to consider our assumptions, what we demand of particular spaces and what can happen in them.

Setting and attention: three interiors in *Reservoir Dogs*

The three interiors that I shall consider here are the café with which the film begins, the warehouse (as it is called in the screenplay) that is the setting of most of the film and with which it ends, and briefly the set of Joe Cabot's Office.

Reservoir Dogs opens with a fade-in from black, to find a conversation between a number of men sitting at a table. The camera, at a height at or a little below the shoulders of the seated men, prowls around and just behind their table, like a big, inquisitive dog. As we listen and watch, the sense of a point of view that circles but always looks across the table is emphasised in the frequent interruption of our gaze by the backs or arms of those on the nearer side. We pick up, from the minimal detail in the background, confirmation that we are in a café: a customer is glimpsed paying and leaving, and there is a brief sight of the first of Tarantino's waitresses, but no clear establishment of a geography that would include a number of other tables and other patrons. (Tarantino shot but chose not to use more extensive footage involving a waitress, according to Jami Bernard (1995, p.177).) The emphasis is on our closeness to the group of men. Our point of view is tightly focused on the one table, effectively if not literally in a corner (we do not have quite enough of a sense of the geography of the place to tell; an exemplary instance of the opposite case, the establishment of a more overt geography, is the shot of Freddy entering a coffee shop to meet Holdaway (Randy Brooks), later in the film). As the conversation continues and we settle into the scene, the camera ceases so obviously to prowl, and concentrates more on shots of the speakers, though still very firmly viewing them from across the table, the frame frequently including an out-of-focus profile or the corner of a jacket from the nearer side. Finally, Joe stands over the table to collect the money, and we are given a more substantial shot of the café, one that is repeated as the sequence ends with the men leaving the table.

We could sum up the function of the direction here by saying that it tells us that none of these men are paying attention to where they are. What the style expresses is something about the special nature of the occasion (which is significant, as on a first viewing we do not yet quite understand what it is), the nervousness and anticipation of it, the sense of the men being disabled from, or not interested in, noticing anything other than the immediate presence of the rest of the group. Here is attention focused towards a collective purpose and expressed in an inward-looking circle, soon to be broken into the loose groupings of the walk towards the cars that forms the background to the credit sequence.

I want now to connect this with the treatment of the warehouse where the greater part of the remaining action, apart from flashbacks, will take place. There are two preliminary distinctions between the warehouse and the café. One connects with Tarantino's control of our point of view. In the café he associated us with the group so that we were no more able to look around us than they were. In the warehouse the point of view detaches us from them – we look on from a distance like an invisible third party. The other distinction is that where the café was a generic setting with almost no distinction (that we could detect), the warehouse opens up the possibility that it is not just an anonymous space, but a carefully posed setting that may act as a commentary on what will happen in it. We can see more, and be more attentive to what we see.

Tarantino's screenplay introduces the warehouse with the direction: 'The camera does a 360 around an empty warehouse.' But the opposite is the case in the film. Not only is there no such shot, but a dynamic of the following sequences is to reveal the space of the warehouse and its function only gradually to us.

There is no establishing exterior shot of the building. The first shot is from inside, as Larry bursts in with the injured Freddy, and of the door bearing an enigmatic sign: the letters 'KING'. Perhaps we are already being offered a small, possibly unintended, gag about partial revelations: we learn much later that the letters are part of a banal message, NO PARKING. What follows shows us little apart from a few glimpses of shapes and textures. The camera is held closely on Freddy and Larry, as Freddy lies collapsed on the ramp where he and Larry will be found at the end of the film. This camerawork continues for all of the next part of their dialogue, expressing, or revealing, the indifference of the two men to the space.

We are given a wider shot of half of the main chamber of the warehouse only on the entry of a third party, Mr Pink. Now we see something that looks rather like a stage, a conventional theatrical setting – a squarish space with exits to left and right and at the rear the archway leading from the ramp on which Freddy lies. At the centre rear are a group of objects: a dustbin, a number of folding chairs, a toilet bowl and cistern which seem disconnected, and a ladder. A couple of chains hang from beams in the ceiling. The whole looks as if we are being invited to read it as if we were the audience of a modern play, or a classic performed in a modishly empty space. It is not too difficult to draw a conclusion that we are seeing a fairly simple representation of the discarded. The conjunction of dustbin and toilet seems to offer a thought about waste or debris, if we want to be more specific.

But the film is teasing us, or rather playing with our desire to grasp the meanings of its spaces. As Larry and Mr Pink leave Freddy in the main chamber and retreat to another room to clean themselves up and discuss their situation, the camera first seems just to repeat (or we might feel, to overemphasise) the 'waste' motif, showing us a broken, discarded toilet seat, a piece of sanitary ware, a rubbish bin and a sink plunger. But then, in an uninterrupted movement, it takes up a position in medium longshot, showing us a corridor at the end of which we see Larry and Mr Pink conversing. To the left of this corridor some white robes are hanging. Tarantino seems to hold this relatively restrained, unusual camera position for longer than we might expect before going to a set-up in the room with the two men, as if he wants us to notice, or even wonder about, these garments. Are they gowns, or protective coats?

When we enter the room, we see it is dressed with another range of objects, subtly different from the first – hoses, a machine of some kind, containers of some sort of liquid. As Larry and Mr Pink talk, we might note that the wall behind their heads is tiled from floor to ceiling. This is some kind of a washroom, and evidently not a kitchen. As he paces around, we see another partially revealed sign next to a machine on the wall here '. . . USE'. We also see, behind Mr Pink, that the cladding is missing from part of one wall, so whatever is involved here does not necessarily call for the place to be particularly sterile.

This is of course not a particularly difficult set of images to read, and as the data accumulates we slowly grasp that the building is (or possibly was?) a morgue, and the machinery and accessories we have seen are to do with the preparation of the dead for burial. The confirmation comes when we return to the main chamber. As Larry and Mr Pink go into their Mexican stand-off, the camera slowly tracks back, revealing, just before it reaches Mr Blonde, the side of a tall, wrapped object, which is, just explicitly enough so that we can notice it if we like, a coffin. The immediately subsequent set-ups in the next few sequences do not repeat the image, however. We wait until Blonde's (appropriate and premonitory) line, 'Nobody's going anywhere,' for the camera to reveal that there are several coffins, variously more or less disguised by their coverings, on this side of the chamber, standing upright on wooden pallets. The coffins, and another wrapped or shrouded object, which is possibly a hearse, on which Mr Blonde perches, will figure intermittently in the rest of the film. They are present until the final Mexican stand-off takes place, and Joe and Nice Guy die: at this point the camerawork again closes in on Freddy and Larry on the ramp, and Tarantino concludes the film with a two-shot, then a single shot of Larry, and finally the empty space which his falling body has just vacated. (Jeff Dawson (1995, p.60) quotes Sandy Reynolds-Wasco, the film's set decorator, describing the set as 'the back of a funeral parlour', and states that it was in fact a disused mortuary.)

It would be possible to see the morgue setting as a simple layer of supporting imagery, a relatively crude *memento mori* to accompany the deadly events of Tarantino's narrative. But how clearly, and by whom, is it perceived? It is relatively easy for the film's audience either to ignore or to fail to notice it, or to enjoy it as a process of gradual, nicely paced revelation. A parallel question can be applied to the participants in the narrative, who are arguably always aware of what is in the warehouse and what it is used for, and have had a chance to see it whole from the start of the caper. (It is where the planning meeting takes place – the coffins appear in that flashback.) But none of them appear at any point to notice it or to think it worth commenting on, as if the whole function of the place were irrelevant to them or outside the scope of their attention. They are so profoundly detached from the world that they have no way of perceiving where they are.

These issues can be focused by considering my third interior, the set of Joe's office. Its framed map of a famous mercantile empire (Venice), the globe on the desk, the elephant's foot and most of all the prominent set of tusks that frame the figure of Joe at his desk: these are Tarantino's way of asserting that there can also be circumstances in which a character expresses meaning through the design of his space. We can reasonably suppose Joe to have chosen this decor; a man who thinks of himself as a kind of modern prince or empire builder might come up with something like this.

My conclusion from these three examples is that Tarantino wants to foreground the significance of attention (and of inattentiveness, or inability to attend). He wants us to see that we, or the characters in his narrative, can be clearly aware, or sublimely unaware, of the meanings of objects in the spaces we inhabit (or in the narratives we watch) according to where and how our attention is fixed. Any element of an interior can be what we see that a character chooses or creates, or can be a puzzle that we might see but that the characters seem unable to see, unable to know what they are looking for. (I take the 'Rosebud' sled in *Citizen Kane* to be cinema's most famous example of this.) The most important thing about the coffee shop, the warehouse setting and the office is not what is revealed, but how it is noticed or ignored, and by whom.

Pulp Fiction and the detached private house

In *Reservoir Dogs*, Tarantino never takes us into a domestic space, that is to say, into a space that somebody would reliably call their home. We come nearest to it with Joe Cabot and with Freddy, but what we see in the relevant scenes with Joe suggest only that this is an office, and the one sequence in Freddy's apartment carries the implication that the place is part of his cover story, that it is exactly not where he usually lives. (This is, of course, related to the character of the male group, which I have discussed at length in Chapter 1.)

The emphasis in *Pulp Fiction* is the opposite: it is full of the homely. We are presented early on with a marginal or failed attempt at it, the apartment in which Brett and his friends are staying. Later we are taken into places that are unmistakably homes, the houses inhabited by Lance (Eric Stoltz) and

Jody (Rosanna Arquette), Marcellus and Mia Wallace, Jimmie and Bonnie (Vanessa Valentino). There are two further heterosexual couples. One, implicitly not married, seems stranded, at least in terms of this film's narrative, in one place: this is Pumpkin (Tim Roth) and Honey Bunny (Amanda Plummer), in the restaurant where their botched robbery bookends the film. The other, Butch and Fabienne, are arguably a lot closer to a relationship that looks or feels like marriage, or something that might turn into one. They work out their story in a series of temporary or sterile or otherwise unsatisfactory places, not inappropriate for a man whose identity is in part, as I have analysed elsewhere, unhappily entangled with a narrative of the past.

The three domestic spaces of the film that are given extended attention are always associated with the married state, as the script establishes in each case. If this is thought to be an unlikely subject, then we can muse over the fact that it is certainly reflected in the substance of the conversation between Jules and Vincent about Antwan Rocamorra and foot massage that is one of the founding moves of the film. It is essentially a conversation about what is and is not an appropriate form of contact with a married woman.

The build-up to these issues is relatively slow. The film's first instance of violence occurs outside the domestic world altogether, and the second instance outside a successfully realised domestic world. The first, the robbery in the Hawthorne Grill, suggests that even a relatively benign public place may become one of terror. Tarantino annotates this setting in two ways. He photographs it so as to stress the horizontal lines in his widescreen frame (venetian blinds, seating, even Honey Bunny conforming to the shape by a pose in which she leans happily along the table at one point) with the result that the space appears attractive and harmonious. But he also takes a moment to suggest unsatisfactory social relations, showing us that Honey Bunny is too pressingly grateful, and Pumpkin too rude, to the waitress – a nice extension of one of the subjects that opened *Reservoir Dogs*.

If in this benign space the sudden violence seems shockingly strange, the opposite is true of the second instance, the execution of the three boys in the apartment house. What we see of the bare room suggests a failure of the personal or domestic to make an impression, which becomes an appropriate background to barbaric behaviour. We see in Jules a ferocity that takes the form of breaking the conventions appropriate to a proper domestic scene – demanding a bite of the burger and helping himself to Brett's drink.

These settings set up a strong contrast with the first home we see, Lance and Jody's house, described in the screenplay as 'a suburban house in Echo Park'. Should we be in any danger of missing the cosy domestic note, Tarantino opens the sequence wittily with a modern equivalent to an image of sewing as feminine preoccupation in a nineteenth-century novel. This is a conversation between Jody and her friend Trudi (Bronagh Gallagher) on the subject of body piercing, and the importance of the benign domestic icon 'every one of them done with a needle' as opposed to bad technology: 'That gun goes against the entire idea behind piercing.'

The action that follows is Vincent's purchase of heroin from Lance. Lance's drug dealing is presented as an entirely unexceptional activity, carried on in broadly the same terms as if he were selling health food or comic books. In his 'office', which turns out to be the marital bedroom decorated with Indian hangings and Jody's collection of shoes, and photographed from angles that stress the confined space, Lance and Vincent chat while Jody fetches the accessories of drug packaging from the kitchen. They are presented as two not-quite-young men, beginning to bemoan the sad state of present times (someone has damaged Vincent's car) from the perspective of their view of themselves as good, ordinary citizens. (The mood is strongly underlined in a sequence deleted from the final cut, in which Lance is given a monologue complaining that you can't get good directions from a gas station nowadays. The sequence is included as an extra on the DVD.) Dominant here is the note of the homespun, the messy house full of the detritus of ordinary life, and not given over to modern technologies. The dealing in heroin (as opposed to cocaine), Lance's old-fashioned balance (as opposed to a digital weighing machine) and even Vincent's glass syringe, effectively the last image of the sequence, speak to an older world.

Again, there is a sharp contrast with the next domestic setting, which follows almost immediately, as Vincent arrives at the Wallace house to collect Mia and take her out to dinner. The opening image of the entranceway to the house, with its careful assembly of designer plants and posed statuary, suggest a domestic environment expressing considerable wealth, the containment of the energies of the natural world and achieved exact design. It is also, as the next minutes show, highly technologised, with an intercom at first replacing face-to-face conversation, and security monitors rather than TV. In so far as the natural or human is included in it, it is either neatly contained (the vase of flowers) or offered as a setting for an ideal simulacrum of the body (the wire sculpture of the seated figure in the living room). Tarantino includes a standard Hollywood prop, a painting of the woman of the house over the mantelpiece, expressive both of the idealisation of the figure, and a reminder that she, like her portrait, can be thought of as an exquisite, valuable possession.

The move to Jack Rabbit Slim's is a move from private to public space, but otherwise the restaurant is the equivalent to the Wallace house. It is another technologised interior, where rather than windows we see a huge bank of monitors that present an image of movement in an exterior, and again the human figures are ones that suggest either a glossy perfection (some of the other diners) or an imitation of images of perfection (the waiters and waitresses dressed as stars of the past, and particularly as glamour stars: Marilyn Monroe, Mamie Van Doren).

It is Mia who insists on going to Jack Rabbit Slim's despite Vincent's objection, and she clearly knows it, whereas it is new to him. Her desire for familiar environments such as her home and the restaurant is related to her need to dominate or retain control, to believe that she can determine the outcome of the situation. To understand this, we need to think about the plot here.

What is at issue is a narrative familiar from other Hollywood movies: we might have been prompted into recognising it by the sight of the portrait over the mantelpiece, reminding us that this is the marital home of a millionaire. The plot is the absence of the husband, the arrival of a male visitor, a first meeting, and the mutual attraction of the wife and the visitor. The difficulty is how this is to be addressed, given that both parties are aware of the likely consequences of acting on their attraction, as Vincent on his part has been making clear from the beginning of the film.

Jack Rabbit Slim's seems the exactly correct setting for a controlled encounter. While invoking the 1950s, the car-as-table represents paradoxically the opposite of the meaning of the car in its original context. Rather than a closed space for an intimate assignation, it is totally exposed to view, a hard, glossy, extremely public spot in which the diners are rigidly seated at a fixed distance from each other. Another element of control is Mia's use of cocaine, which she snorts before leaving home and again in the Ladies' Room of the restaurant. I believe we are intended to read this as a technique for adjusting mood equivalent to the other high-modern elements of these environments; we could say that cocaine is to heroin as the Wallace home is to the Lance/Jody home.

What works against the control of distance is partly a degree of restless vitality in Mia, expressed in the first shot of her bare feet at home and picked up in her sudden desire to dance in the twist contest. By the time the couple arrive back at the Wallace home it looks as if the intention to keep the flirtation within bounds is unravelling. Mia's finding of the heroin in Vincent's pocket is the result of drifting perilously into comfy intimacy with him – she finds the baggie only because she is wearing his overcoat – only to be interrupted when she mistakes the heroin for cocaine, snorts it, and overdoses.

There is clearly a literal explanation as to why Vincent bundles Mia into the car and drives her to Lance's home, which is that he knows that Lance possesses, or once possessed, the adrenaline shot that might save her life. But what Tarantino does with the sequence that follows makes more of it than this. It becomes a matter of taking Mia into a different world, one that

Pulp Fiction. Perilous intimacy: Mia (Uma Thurman) and Vincent (John Travolta) arrive back at the Wallace home after winning the trophy at Jack Rabbit Slim's. *Source*: British Film Institute.

she would normally never encounter, a world in which the conditions that will save her can be met, conditions that are essentially those of magic, or of a fairy tale.

The linking sequence is important, as offering an image that is relatively unusual for Tarantino: it opens with an exterior long shot of an empty boulevard. Essentially the continuation and summary of the mood of the house and restaurant, the shot offers only the hardness of designed urban space, an elegant composition in greys, as the rainwater reflects on the hard surfaces. Vincent's car shatters this orderliness, skidding into frame on its frantic mission of rescue.

We cut to Lance. In case we have forgotten the homely note, it is reprised; we see him, still in his dressing gown, receiving Vincent's mobile phone call while eating cereal and watching TV. The show is one in which chaos is reigning (we glimpse an actress bringing down a birdcage on her antagonist's head) but with a benign outcome. The one line we hear is, 'I give up, I'll marry you.' Once Mia is inside the building, the note of domestic chaos and routine marital strife is sounded again, as Jody and Lance bicker while he searches through the piles of detritus for his 'medical book' that goes with the adrenaline pack. All is hand-held camera and tight space as the couple rush about, and we see Lance from a point of view just outside the narrow doorway of the room in which the book is lost.

Pulp Fiction. The suburban drug dealer, Lance (Eric Stoltz), talks to Vincent on the phone. In the foreground is the stoned Trudi (Bronagh Gallagher). *Source*: British Film Institute.

It is important that he does not find it. What we are seeing is not a scene of technological cure. Rather, it is something that begins in a mood of manic knockabout, and ends with the enactment of a ritual.

At first the pace of its dialogue seems nearest to a Danny Kaye routine, say the 'chalice from the palace' sequence in *The Court Jester* (Norman Panama, Melvin Frank, 1955). There is the series of exchanges between the two men as to who will give Mia the shot, culminating in this hilarious note:

> LANCE (*moving his arm repeatedly up and down*): You got to bring the needle down, in a stabbing motion.
> VINCENT (*watching*): I got to stab her three times?

There is also an important shift in the cinematic style and the choreography of movement in the sequence. When the search for the book is abandoned, the point of view changes – there are some inserted close-ups, but the key shot has the camera positioned in the doorway to the living room, almost at ground level, looking up into the room with Mia's head in the foreground. The four figures begin to gather around the unconscious woman, Vincent and Lance either side of Mia, Jody and eventually Trudi looking on from behind them. The effect is one of drama, or theatre: an audience at an important ritual. The sense of our looking up at these figures almost as if this were happening on a stage is accentuated by the framing, the columns of the room dividers that appear on either side of the group. There is a sense of gathered attention, expressed both through Jody, who announced the mood by putting on her white dressing gown, as if this were something to be robed up for, and by the stoned Trudi, who has finally moved off her sofa to be a witness of the climax. The needle is plunged into the heart, and the adrenaline, or the magic, does its work. Mia's convulsion scatters the audience. When she has come to rest Tarantino cuts to a medium shot of all five players. The four onlookers simultaneously lean forward to inspect the woken woman, in a perfectly coordinated gesture of anxious enquiry.

What is Tarantino suggesting? He wants to divorce this act of saving a life from its pathological literals, to take it away from science and give it back to people who believe in the scenarios that movies can offer, can make come true. Perhaps only people who can sufficiently confuse fantasy with reality can make Mia come to life again. Rather than a place that believes in, or depends on, medical technologies (as might be, the Wallace house), he takes us back to a place where stabbing Mia in the heart can be a benign version of the 'whole idea of piercing' (which is where we came in to this particular world).

There are many ways in which the contrast between these two settings can be annotated, but it may be most helpful here to conclude by setting them out as a table, which includes both the distinctions I have discussed and some others.

Lance and Jody's house	The Wallace house
Chaotic piles of objects	Carefully posed objects
Heroin	Cocaine
Colour	Black/white
Confined spaces	Open, elegant spaces
Television	Surveillance monitors
Quarrelsomeness	Repression
Child art (stuck on the screen of a broken TV)	The portrait of Mia
Texture: cloth, terry towelling (Jody's robe)	Texture: hard surfaces (glass, metal)
The stoned Trudi	The wire sculpture
The happy conjunction of flesh and metal (piercing with a needle, stabbing Mia)	The careful separation of flesh and metal (Mia's lips not touching the microphone)

In the light of these distinctions, I want to move on to the final marital home, that of Jimmie and Bonnie, the place in which Vincent and Jules take refuge when they have the problem of the disposal of their bloodied car and the remains of Marvin.

The quality of Jimmie's home can be immediately located through its drug of choice: where we have seen heroin and then cocaine, here we have coffee. Associated neither with small-time crime and the threat of exposure (Lance) nor with big-time crime and the evidences of power (Marcellus), the note here is that of the ordinary: Bonnie is a nurse on shift work and Jimmie, whose occupation we never learn, takes pride in his gourmet coffee that is the decriminalised version of Lance and his pride in his quality heroin. There is, typically for Tarantino, no establishing shot of the house or even one of Jimmie: the sequence begins with its subject, with the image of the basin in which Vincent and Jules are washing their hands. Eventually, in the shot that announces the arrival of the Wolf in his Porsche, we see a pleasant, wide, suburban street. The house itself is distinctive only in that it is orderly and neat, neither chaotic nor plutocratic. The presentation of it stresses the natural light and openness to the outside.

Our most extensive exposure to the interior of the house is during Jules' phone call to Marcellus. Tarantino gives us a fantasy sequence in which Jules imagines Bonnie coming home and finding 'a load of gangsters doing gangster shit' in her house. As the camera follows Bonnie making her way through the living room, we observe not only its neatness but the absence of the modern. Not only is there no surveillance equipment, there is no TV, and the first object we glimpse through the doorway is actually a piano. The effect is to associate Jimmie and Bonnie with the pieties of earlier generations, a world that observes the importance of the marriage bond and the necessity of not disturbing a wife. This can be connected to Jimmie's assumption of the role of good husband, particularly his speech to Jules: 'There isn't anything you can say that will make me forget I love my wife.'

These notes suggest that we can now trace a movement through the film in terms of its representation of marriages and homes. After two sequences that oppose a simple activity like eating breakfast with violence (you are enjoying your breakfast grill, and you are robbed; you are enjoying your breakfast burger, and you are shot to death) we move to the home as sympathetic or familiar, where your needs can be met and you can share your world view with like-minded companions. Like Lance and Jody's arguments, it is energetically disorderly, but not radically threatening. The shift to the millionaire's home is (it seems almost always the case in Hollywood film) a negative one, to a place governed by repression and commodification, and hopeless fantasies of rescuing a trapped princess.

The return to Lance's house recognises that it contains the possibility of saving a life, of a kind of ideal form of action, where a fantasy might come true. From there the move to Jimmie's home is a move from night and fantasy to day and reality, to an ordinary, ordered world that must be kept clean, free of 'gangster shit' (and gangster blood).

Clean the car, clean the gangsters, have it all done by the time Bonnie comes home. The tone seems to be that of a triumphant escapade in domestic comedy, a crisis solved in suburbia, a wife who will never know and a marriage that will be undisturbed. The residue of unease from the episode is captured in the suggestion of the convenience, to our consciences, of not allowing ourselves to see something, or to admit that we are seeing it. In Jules' fantasy of the thing that must not happen, Bonnie walks in on the three men holding the dead body of Marvin. We know that this is not a likely scenario, as there is no reason to bring the corpse into the house, but it is significant that he imagines disaster as an act of seeing. Connect this with Jimmie's angry rhetoric at the beginning of the episode about Jules not seeing the sign on his house reading 'Dead nigger storage', which may be an uneasy admission that he acknowledges the brutality of what is afoot even as he repudiates it.

What this seems to be arguing is that these actions can only be made possible by an act of collective refusal to face the implications that underlie them. These are the expendability of a young black man's life and implicitly the reach of this violence into the lives of Jimmie and Bonnie if things don't go to plan. It is necessary – or, rather, it is essential – to pretend that Jimmie and Jules are just 'buddies', that all this is just some kind of harmless fun. In the screenplay, the point is made at still greater length by an extension of the hosing down sequence in the backyard, in which Jimmie insists on taking a snapshot of the three gangsters.

Tarantino ensures that some uneasiness persists into the rest of the film regarding what lies beneath assumptions about cleaning up the dirty. The idea of how far our behaviour is and is not affected by the imagination of dirt, specifically shit, is taken into another context and pursued in the breakfast table conversation between Jules and Vincent about bacon, pigs and dogs that follows this episode and introduces the final minutes of the action.

I shall end with the sequence with Jimmie and the Wolf in Jimmie's bedroom, which successfully captures the combination of uneasiness and the quotidian. Tarantino holds for a long time the shot through the bedroom doorway, emphasising the narrow spaces and common objects of the home. Jimmie demurs regarding the use to which his best linen is being put – to conceal the remaining blood on the seats of the car. He invokes the family circle, that the linen was a wedding present from his Uncle Conrad and Aunt Ginny, who 'aren't with us any more'. The lame phrase is answered by an act of redescribing the family, dislodging the late uncle and aunt (who were not millionaires) and inventing 'your Uncle Marcellus' (who is). The Wolf peels off a stack of banknotes, while enquiring of Jimmy, 'I like oak myself, that's what's in my bedroom. How 'bout you, Jimmie, you an oak man?'

The comic tone is successfully sustained, but the nervous bleat with which Tarantino performs Jimmy's reply, 'oak's nice', suggests what has to be ignored in his assent to this transaction. So this is a world that purchases its idea of itself as ordinary at the price of a refusal to face the violence around it – although perhaps Tarantino would argue that this is exactly what the ordinary world actually does.

Street life: *Jackie Brown*'s wide open spaces

Jackie Brown, as the use of the name of a single figure for its title suggests, is a film that does not address the couple and their domestic space, in sharp contrast to *Pulp Fiction*. There are no marriages here, nor couples who feel as if they are anywhere very close to that condition. There are relationships of convenience that have a more or a less explicit sexual dimension (Ordell and Melanie, Ordell and his other girls). There is a relationship that approaches but does not quite reach a point of stated sexual interest (Nicolet and Jackie). At the centre of the narrative is a romance (Max and Jackie), but it is one that does not quite develop into an evident affair. It transmutes into a partnership, and finally melts away in the film's last scene.

The film opens with a shot of a space that is technically an interior, one through which the heroine moves alone, her gaze fixed on nothing, conscious of the possibility that she might be the object of the casual or attentive observing eye. The woman is not called on to return or to detect a gaze: that is an advantage of the size and nature of the space around her. This is the only one of these three films to open with a single figure, and the only one not initially set in a clearly enclosed, interior space. Alongside this we can put the fact that *Jackie Brown* moves its characters, often shown alone, through a series of more or less impersonal urban locales. A list, in roughly descending order of size, gives us LAX Airport, Del Amo Mall, a multi-storey car park, a courtroom, a record store, a prison holding cell, the offices of Cherry Bail Bonds, the offices and an interrogation room in a police station. Finally there are three specific small spaces, which are certainly private but which we can immediately recognise as ones that impress their impersonality on us: a fitting room in a department store, the toilet in the bail bond office, and a toilet in a plane.

Jackie Brown. Achieving her ends by knowing how to behave in public spaces: Jackie (Pam Grier) on her way to make the money drop. *Source*: British Film Institute.

Jackie Brown is in part about the ability of a single figure to conduct herself, to achieve her ends by knowing both how to behave in these public spaces and how to manipulate the behaviour of others in them. Consider again the meaning of the credit sequence shots of Jackie in the airport. What they tell us is that she is a public performer, well aware as a career stewardess that she is an object on show (her bright blue uniform under-lines the point) and more than capable of knowing how to respond to public challenge by men. (This is demonstrated by her composure during the scene in which she is first stopped in the car park by Nicolet and Vargas.)

Compare this with a subsequent sequence that involves an open space, Ordell's execution of Beaumont. The difference is that while Ordell's control and composure is striking (I discussed this in Chapter 2) the world that he dominates is that of the dark, and the space is one that is socially empty, the waste ground where Beaumont is killed. We might connect this to the scene near the end of the film in which Louis shoots Melanie in the nearly deserted car park of the mall. Both are scenes in which a character (Beaumont, Melanie) has to be coerced into leaving a house in order reluctantly to carry out a cooperative operation. In both cases this reluctant partner is killed shortly afterwards in a suitably quiet spot.

The distinction between the different kinds of wide open spaces in which Jackie and Ordell feel in control must be borne in mind when we consider the latter half of the film and the action that takes place in Del Amo mall. The Mall, the 'largest indoor mall in the world' as the establishing title shot tells us, is a familiar complex devoted to the sale of commodities and to various kinds of refreshment. We might say it is rather like the similar environment in an airport. Both reflect back to Jackie's role as stewardess for Cabo Air, which is (as she points out elsewhere) a form of salesgirl/ waitress. Hence her awareness of both selling commodities and her own commodified status. Comparatively, Ordell is out of place here. Lurking in a store doorway as he observes the meeting between Max and Jackie, it is clear that the mall is the space where he feels most disempowered. Ordell likes bars, cars, and the houses he owns or controls.

Jackie's confidence is related to the degree to which this space is gendered, one where women are seen to possess familiarity and control. The money exchange, as we see it take place in the 'trial run' sequence in the mall, is an exchange between two women involving shopping bags. Tarantino works in details with both Ordell (forgetting to pick up the Billingsley bag) and later with Nicolet (having trouble describing it) that speak to the gender politics of these accessories, and the anxiety they induce in these men. If we think of it as set up in this way, the reading of the final exchange sequence is not difficult.

It begins with a variant of the opening shot. This is the moment in which Jackie walks into the mall, the bright blue now transferred from her uniform to the brilliant background tiles. The note of confidence and possession of the space is further sounded through the soundtrack, Randy Crawford singing 'Street Life'.

The further gendering of the exchange is effected in moving it from the relatively public setting of the snack bar of the 'trial run' to a yet more exclusively gendered place, the women's clothes store, and to an annex normally prohibited to men, the fitting room. Tarantino makes sure that we register the assumptions that Jackie and Max are playing to. The presence of a man looking at women's clothes in the absence of a partner is addressed in the brief scene in which a salesgirl questions him (of course in the mode of being helpful) and tells him 'don't be shy' in response to his establish- ment of his role: that he is waiting for his wife. Jackie creates an appropriate mood in her friendly exchanges with another woman in charge of gendered space: the salesgirl, Amy (Aimee Graham). The scene ends with two nicely placed pieces of performance: Jackie pretending to be the panicking woman as she runs through the mall and finally shouts for Nicolet, and Max, extending his act as the married bourgeois, collecting the bag of beach towels (now containing $500,000) from the fitting room. These scams work so well because they seem so 'natural'. Nicolet has no trouble in believing that an apparently competent woman asked to perform a

Jackie Brown. Telling a salesgirl in the clothes store that he is waiting for his wife, Max Cherry (Robert Foster) observes Jackie from a distance in the crucial moments of the money-drop sequence. *Source*: British Film Institute.

complex task will break down and panic when it goes wrong. Similarly a middle-aged, inoffensive white male needs to express just the right blend of caution and prerogative when asking Amy's permission to enter the ladies' fitting room. Thus the whole of the money exchange emphasises principally Jackie's control of this kind of commercial space, and her ability to manipulate assumptions about behaviour in it.

Finally, I shall look at a single image. This is of a threshold and hence of the relation between inside and out, and the possibilities implied by the world of the street and the world of the impersonal interior. It is an image that Tarantino repeats, a shot of the street taken through the window of the Cherry Bail Bond office, the prominent signwriting on the window drawing our attention to the hard, transparent barrier. (In its slightly old-fashioned feel, it seems to recollect windows in Westerns. We might compare it with the use made of the window of 'The Shinbone Star' in *The Man Who Shot Liberty Valance*, as marking the boundary between the wide, open spaces where part of the life of the world is conducted, and the enclosed office space where it is mediated, turned into words, by men who have committed themselves to that business.)

What Tarantino does is to reverse the traditional trope, endlessly explored in Westerns, in which the woman is contained by the interior while the man possesses the freedom to wander. The film uses the threshold twice. We first see it when Ordell visits Max's office, accompanied by Louis. The bail bond office makes the disoriented Louis uneasy, and he does not want to wait outside. To return to the car involves facing strange novel technologies: how a modern car is unlocked, which Ordell has to explain to him. Tarantino devotes some space to this, the camera even following Louis out into the street, a moment that would be redundant but for its underlining of the man's uneasiness with the outside. (This is the man who will later respond to being lost in a car park by shooting his companion.)

The second use of the image announces the closing action of the film. Jackie arrives, in the same car, to bid Max farewell. Her easy movement between car, street and office complements the suggestion that it is the figure of Max who is trapped, who has in Jackie's words 'a business to run', who will not be the party to be returned to. Only Jackie can be seen to achieve some kind of freedom, and Tarantino expresses this by taking us to a favourite location, the interior of a moving car. Here it is presented for a moment as utopian, a perfect performance space in which Jackie mouths the words as Bobby Womack performs '110th Street' on the car stereo as we fade out.

Reflecting on these explorations, what is most striking is Tarantino's remarkable range, expressed in the shifts between the films. *Reservoir Dogs* is the story of men radically disconnected from the world around them, no more able to consider its significance than the men throwing the junk into Charles Foster Kane's furnace. *Pulp Fiction* offers a range of couples, their spaces and their strange durability; we might note that all five heterosexual couples survive the events of this film. *Jackie Brown* shows a world in which romance is not quite possible, but one in which an independent woman can dominate open space sufficiently to survive a tale of death and entrapment.

In terms of the association of space with freedom, we begin with the claustrophobia of *Reservoir Dogs* where the world outside the room seems progressively to cease to exist (the shades of Sartre's *Huis Clos* and Vian's *The Empire Builders* are not too distant). We move to the end(s) of *Pulp Fiction*, where Butch and Fabienne's roaring off into their future on Zed's chopper is concealed inside the movie, which instead concludes with Jules and Vincent acknowledging that it's time to go and bowing politely off stage. Finally, in *Jackie Brown* we have the ending at the end, as Jackie drives off into a new world. But she is alone – which might remind us of the original ending written by Tarantino for *True Romance*.

6 Adaptation: Tarantino, Paul Schrader and Elmore Leonard

I am conscious that little of what I have so far had to say about *Jackie Brown* has addressed one of its distinguishing qualities, that it is (as yet) unique in Tarantino's main work in being an adaptation of a literary source rather than an original screenplay. In this chapter I want to consider the matter of adaptation, and to do this by placing another adaptation alongside Tarantino's film, one produced in the same year as *Jackie Brown*, and derived from a different novel by the same author: Paul Schrader's *Touch*, based on Elmore Leonard's novel of the same name.

There are some respects in which this is an oblique comparison. There is a wide difference in experience and point in career: *Jackie Brown* is Tarantino's third film, *Touch* Schrader's eleventh. The novels are of apparently different genres and have very different histories. *Rum Punch*, from which *Jackie Brown* is derived, is an American crime novel in the mainstream of Leonard's work. It was published in the USA in 1992 only five years before the film appeared, suggesting that it was immediately considered as a possible project. This is unsurprising in the light of the track record of Leonard's crime work up to that point, films derived from a number of novels, including *52 Pick-Up* (1974), *Cat Chaser* (1982) and *Get Shorty* (1991). (According to Jami Bernard (1995, p.265), Miramax purchased the rights to four of Leonard's novels at about this time.)

Touch is about a miracle worker, about 'mystical things happening to an ordinary person in a contemporary setting'. In its interest in the space occupied by religious practices and their fate in a culture of commodities, it can be aligned with a number of major American works, including Sinclair Lewis' *Elmer Gantry* (1927, filmed by Richard Brooks in 1980) and Frank Capra's *The Miracle Woman* (1932), as well as elements of Nathanael West's *The Day of the Locust* (1939, filmed by John Schlesinger in 1975). In his preface to *Touch*, from which the words above are quoted, Leonard lays out its history for us. Written and submitted for publication in 1977, it was clearly felt to be an unacceptable commercial risk by Leonard's publishers.

The rights to the novel were returned to him in 1982. It was offered to another publisher, and finally appeared in 1987. The 'off-trail' nature of the material, to quote Leonard's term, is again reflected in the further decade that passed before Schrader's 1997 film.

A major reason for looking at Tarantino and Schrader together is that both come to adaptation with a history of writing distinguished original screenplays filmed both by themselves and by others. I shall not repeat the details of Tarantino's career: a selection of Schrader's work shows him directing his own original scripts (*Hardcore* 1978, *American Gigolo* 1979, *Light Sleeper* 1992), and filming scripts that he has adapted from other sources (*Blue Collar* 1977, *Affliction* 1997). His work with other directors includes both an original script for a famous film (*Taxi Driver*, Martin Scorsese, 1975) and adaptations (*The Mosquito Coast*, Peter Weir, 1986, and *Raging Bull* and *The Last Temptation of Christ*, both directed by Martin Scorsese in 1980 and 1988 respectively). The experience is (evidently, because the career is longer) greater in Schrader's case, but we might expect both these accomplished writers to have a clear sense of what it is they wish to derive from their source material. We can ask if the particular directions in which they take it can illuminate something about the different, although not unrecognisably remote, American worlds of the two films.

Rather than looking immediately at the two novels and their respective adaptations, it may be helpful to begin with Elmore Leonard. Leonard's work has two apparent points of reference in terms of genre: the Western, and the urban crime thriller. There are early Western novels (beginning with *The Bounty Hunters* in 1953) and screenplays (*Joe Kidd*, 1972) and the urban thrillers that are a major part of his work from the 1980s onwards. This is not a straightforward change of direction, although no doubt Leonard was responding to commercial pressures as the Western began to decline.

Engaging densely with the Western from the 1950s to the 1970s, Leonard understands its archetypes and narratives as increasingly problematic. (I have discussed these issues as they appear in the first Western with an original screenplay written by Leonard, John Sturges' *Joe Kidd*, in my *Clint Eastwood: Actor and Director*.) Rather than shifting between one genre and another, Leonard can be thought of as inserting the figures and impulses of the late Western into the world of urban crime. Here they become no less problematic, but rather produce a series of demands and models for male behaviour (and for relations between men and women) that are in most respects negative and damaging. An exemplary text is his 1980 novel *City Primeval: High Noon in Detroit* (the book appears to have lost its subtitle in its English edition). *City Primeval* is a crime thriller in which the protagonist and antagonist conceive their roles explicitly in terms of a Western shoot-out between rivals, and in which the cop hero is trapped between his image of himself as a modern Wyatt Earp and the realities of urban homicide.

So if we ask what, despite their considerable divergence in genre and subject, the novels *Touch* and *Rum Punch* have in common, we might look for figures who evoke the stereotypes that populate the Western. We can then consider the terms in which such figures function, or are superseded, in the novels' accounts of the relations between the sexes.

An important part of what the novels have in common is generic: a love story. Both conclude with a couple (although in neither case is this where Leonard chooses to begin) and an image of departure. The narrative has followed the woman of the couple from living alone into a relationship with a new man, that is, one she has met in this narrative. In the case of *Touch*, the woman has already happily departed with the man as the last details of the plot are tied up. In the case of *Rum Punch*, the novel ends with the woman leaving the city (and the country) and with a question that is nearly, but not quite, answered: can the couple have a future or not?

Consider the biographies of the two heroines. Lynn Marie Faulkner (*Touch*) is a former baton twirler with two seasons with a religious revival show, which she left at 19 in order to get married. She is divorced, after nine years of marriage, from a Western hero gone to seed: 'behind that rawhide hell-rider image was usually a half-drunk, stove-up . . . freak' (*Touch*, 1988, p.22). Her divorce is followed by a couple of insignificant affairs with men – or affairs with insignificant men – that lead nowhere. She is around 29 years old.

The comparable figure in *Rum Punch* is Jackie Burke, who becomes the Jackie Brown of Tarantino's screenplay. Almost the first thing that we learn about her in the novel is that she is 44 years old. She has been married three times: once, at 19, to a man killed five months later while performing a motorbike stunt while drunk. Her second husband, a pilot, was a Vietnam veteran and hooked on drugs, and her third another drunk – 'the dirt biker come back to life' – who committed suicide.

What is common to these accounts can be summed up in a line that Leonard gives to Jackie and that Tarantino preserves in his film: 'I feel like I'm always starting over.' What Leonard stresses in the cases of both Jackie and Lynn is that these are the second acts of American lives, and that the women cannot see any kind of future before them. Both biographies involve a disastrous commitment to a stereotype of the Western action hero that is already (self-)defeated, and a progressive sense of having little chance, or expectation, of finding a man who is any kind of improvement on the past.

The novels find very different solutions to this situation. In *Touch*, it is the introduction of an entirely different kind of man. Juvenal, who becomes Lynn's lover, is an ex-priest who has spent seven years in a religious order in South America and has the gift of healing. At times he develops the stigmata, and bleeds from his wounds. (In his periodic bleeding, and in his transmission of life from his body, it is easy to see the conception of the figure as a challenge to conventional ideas of masculinity. Schrader introduces a little gag about this into his film, involving what kinds of blood you might find yourself washing off clothing, which seems to associate stigmatic and menstrual bleeding.)

Juvenal is attractive to Lynn because he is so substantially outside the circuits of contemporary life. The repeated note in their affair is a kind of uncertainty as to whether their behaviour as a couple has any relation to the world around them and whether this matters: the creation of a temporarily separate world, one of tenderness and (relative) sexual innocence. Perhaps Leonard is being gently ironic with us here, implying that the possibility of contemporary Americans finding such behaviour available to them is as much a miracle as the healing and the appearance of the stigmata.

Max Cherry in *Rum Punch* is altogether more familiar, related to the stereotypes of the Western and the hard-boiled crime genre, a figure analogous to the older, experienced lawman or the good private eye. His is also a life that has come to a standstill. Leonard sketches the last moves in the disintegration of his marriage and shows him as a weary veteran of 19 years in the bail bond business, 'an expert at waiting' (*Rum Punch*, 1993, p.106). He is 57 years old. Thinking of Jackie and Max's sexual histories we might see them as victims, both of them seduced by what society thought of in earlier times as glamorous qualities that could be incarnated in a sexual partner: respectively the Westerner, and the alternative culture of the 1960s. (Leonard gives us a passage in which Max, musing on his marriage, recalls reading the beat poets to his wife.)

For Max to win Jackie, he has to be a successful version of the action hero in the modern city, and Leonard dramatises this. The book includes a passage in which Max visits Simone and Louis Gara, locates money they are holding for Ordell, and calmly takes an amount that is owed to him, a scene in which he is at his closest to the confident, cool hero. This is followed by a scene with Jackie, in which her realisation that he has taken this money and thus that he might be decisive and collected enough to pull off a much larger robbery, contributes to a mutual seduction that ends with their making love for the first time.

In both *Touch* and *Rum Punch* the stress on the couple's successful physical lovemaking is significant. In *Touch* it is part of the intimacy that renders the lovers apparently almost impregnable to the world around them, and that enables them to escape it at the end. In *Rum Punch* it is a positive element in play within Leonard's ending, in which Max and Jackie's awareness of their suitability for each other is faced with a challenge. They must accept that their relationship might be based on the dominance of the woman rather than the man. In the closing scene Jackie's offer to Max is, 'I'll take you away from all this,' classically, of course, the offer made by the man to the woman at the end of a romance. Their final exchange (Max: 'Where would we go?' Jackie: 'I don't know . . . does it matter?') again reverses the conventional gender roles, while evoking the moment in which a couple conventionally record that they are going to whatever, or wherever, they call home. But the strong possibility is implied in these closing lines that they will overcome this problem.

We might sum this up by saying that in both cases Leonard is interested in the possibility of triumph over the hard conditions in which romance has to exist in these worlds. In both cases the lovers are posed against figures who express the condition of that world, the threat of it. The primary figures, Bill Hill in *Touch* and Ordell Robbie in *Rum Punch*, are of course very different in ways dictated by the mode of each novel, but they could be seen as respectively benign and malign forms of another American archetype, the salesman/con-man. Both of them are dandies, in neither case does sexual activity seem very important to them, and both of them seem to have found that their successful role is when they are men with something to sell. Bearing in mind these elements of comparison and difference, we can now turn to what Schrader and Tarantino make of these materials.

What Tarantino wants to extract from *Rum Punch* is indicated by his change of title. *Jackie Brown* becomes Jackie's story; the centre of the film is the question of what she can do with her life, whether she can be brave and intelligent (and lucky) enough to change it for the better. The question is recast and made specific by what is often thought of as the most significant change in adapting the book. The white Jackie Burke of the novel becomes the black Jackie Brown, so asking this question of a '44-year-old black woman'. (The phrase, intended to demean, is used by the police in Jackie's first interrogation.) I shall return to the subject of Jackie's race, but first let us look at how the focus on the heroine determines Tarantino's choice of materials from the book.

Tarantino announces Jackie's central role with a scene that has no equivalent in *Rum Punch*, the credit sequence in which we watch Jackie move through the airport to board her flight, which I have discussed elsewhere. The opening of the novel, which is not used anywhere in the film, is one in which Ordell introduces Louis, newly released from prison, to an American crowd: they are attending, or rather, they are spectators at a neo-Nazi rally. The decision not to use this is not perhaps just a matter of Tarantino focusing on Jackie rather than Ordell (although it is certainly that) but also of a very different relation to public space and the crowd. Leonard wants to establish Ordell's sense of confidence in his place in this particular public world through representing his ease in a crowd. Tarantino seems not to have any great interest in how an individual feels being in, or looking on at, a crowd – in fact, scenes of a public occasion at which the hero is a spectator are absent so far from his work.

Tarantino goes on to discard areas of material that relate primarily to Ordell and have little or nothing to do with Jackie. They are (a) a sub-plot involving Ordell and Gerald, a neo-Nazi, which is initiated in this abandoned opening scene at the rally, and (b) material to do with Ordell and the 'jackboys', black drug addicts that he uses to do errands. There are other areas that are either excised or less emphasised. Less is made in *Jackie Brown* than in *Rum Punch* of the relationship between Max and his assistant Winston, and of that between the two cop buddies, Nicolet and Dargus (Michael Bowen). A sub-plot involving one of Ordell's jackboys, who shoots Tyler (the cop who is renamed Dargus in the film) and is in turn shot by Nicolet is not used. This can be summed up by saying that a Western-derived interest in male bonds and male groups, which is strongly present in *Rum Punch*, is much less accommodated in the film. Tarantino retains and elaborates various witty sequences of transactions between men (Ordell and Max at the bail bond office, for example, or Ordell and Beaumont) but Ordell and Louis are the only male/male buddies that are substantially retained. Even here, the emphasis is changed. Louis is reimagined for the film with much more stress on his abstractedness and failure to engage coherently with the world outside jail than is the case in the novel, in which he is a more functional and independent figure. Finally, it is indicative that the moment in which a relationship between men is ironically interrogated, Ordell's comment on the picture of Max and Winston (see my discussion on pp.30–1) is an invention of Tarantino's.

In apparent contrast Schrader's film of *Touch* preserves Leonard's title. A reader of the novel presented with the first half hour of exposition in the film might consider, apart from obvious abbreviations and condensations and a few small changes, how little Schrader has intervened in terms of narrative, structure and even dialogue. He starts his film with Leonard's opening scene, an incident of domestic violence that turns into one of healing: Elwin (John Doe), an alcoholic construction worker, strikes his blind wife Virginia (Conchata Ferrell) in a drunken rage. Bill Hill (Christopher Walken), an old friend of Virginia, who once played the organ at his now defunct multifaith church and then Juvenal (Skeet Ulrich), a worker at the Sacred Heart Rehabilitation Center, arrive, and a mystical thing happens to an ordinary person: Virginia's sight is restored. The production credits are played at intervals over this sequence, which ends with Schrader's credit. He then follows the exposition as Leonard presents it, in these sequences, in the same order:

1. Bill Hill at the Rehabilitation Center: he attempts to get in touch with Juvenal.
2. Bill and Lynn Faulkner (Bridget Fonda), who once worked for Bill as a baton twirler and is now a music promoter, in her apartment: Bill puts her up to penetrating the Center by pretending to be an alcoholic.
3. August Murray (Tom Arnold) in court: August, militant leader of a Catholic pressure group for the restoration of traditional rites to the church, demonstrates with his followers.
4. Lynn, Juvenal and August at the Center: Lynn meets Juvenal and they are joined by August, attempting to recruit Juvenal to his cause.
5. Lynn and Juvenal in his office, followed by her seeing him standing in his bedroom, bleeding from his five stigmatic wounds.
6. The dedication of a church: Lynn, Bill Hill and local reporter Kathy Worthington (Janeane Garofalo) in the congregation, August and Juvenal officiating. Juvenal's first public healing, in which he suddenly finds himself, not by his own design, in the position of laying hands on a child. He then flees the scene with Lynn.

There is a direction given to this exposition which has no equivalent in the novel. This is Schrader's use of music, here an insistent, rhythmical electric guitar score by David Grohl that emphasises the energy of move-ment, and underlines the importance in the film of figures who are dealers, promoters, agents, operators, who are at their most alive when in motion. They are the ones seen behind the wheel of a car, but the quality is also marked simply by their purposive walk, which Schrader shows us in a series of shots of characters' feet. This links Bill Hill, August, in part Lynn. It distinguishes them from those who are either unable or unwilling to move (Elwin and Virginia, or the inhabitants of the Center) and from those who are not seen moving, such as Juvenal, who arrives and departs mysteriously in the opening sequence.

This device starts to make the direction of the adaptation clear. Schrader wants to stress not only the contrast between Juvenal's inex-plicable physical gift, which seems to come from another world, and the dealers and promoters in this one, but to celebrate the restlessness, the energetic activeness, of contemporary America. The shot of Bill Hill's boots as he exits his car that is played behind Schrader's credit establishes Bill as a kind of hero for this world, the Western dandy/huckster/con man turned promoter.

In the second half of the film, which follows the scenes I have outlined, the promoter comes into his own. Two sequences demonstrate this, both of which are substantial interventions by Schrader, and are quite unlike anything in the opening half. The first disrupts the film's initial love scene. Juvenal has come to Lynn's apartment, and they fall into each other's arms. In the novel the convention of a paragraph break covers their lovemaking – afterwards they lie nude on Lynn's bed talking to each other. Schrader films both of these scenes, but separates them and inserts into the break, so that it actually sits at the point of the lovemaking, another scene between a man and a woman. This is Bill Hill and Debra Lusanne, a powerful chatshow host with whom Bill is negotiating to sell the rights to Juvenal's first television appearance. Schrader cuts from the pastels and domesticity of Lynn's apartment to the chic modernism of the designer offices at the television station KQRD (chairs of a deep, bright red, a big abstract painting in shades of grey and black, the exposed struts of the building). Gina Gershon as Debra Lusanne is the human embodiment of this design, her perfect turnout poised between attractiveness and intimidation. It seems that what Schrader wants to put to us, expressed through this juxtaposition, is that both couples enjoy kinds of intimacy and understanding of each other. The innocents on the bed and the dealers in the office are both parts of Schrader's America. On the one hand he is observing a culture that marvellously (and famously) holds out the possibility of retrieving some-thing, of starting over, and on the other hand seeing the devotion to the quest for success, and the forms of measuring it, here matters of numbers: of money, and of TV ratings.

The second sequence follows close on this one, and offers a variation that emphasises a similar point. Again it begins with the couple of Lynn and Juvenal. Schrader films a scene in which they make a post-coital meal in her kitchen. The note remains one of discovered innocence or fun, with Lynn wearing minimal clothes (panties and a see-though apron) and Juvenal naked, and the conversation is essentially one about male virginity. All of this follows closely the terms laid out in the novel. But at its close Schrader cuts, as the couple begin to embrace again, to a scene that has no equivalent in Leonard.

It opens with Schrader's signature shot, the guitar score and the image of Bill Hill's boots as he walks into the office of the newspaper where Kathy Worthington is a reporter. He has come to start a negotiation regarding Juvenal's story by giving her a list of books on angels and saints. Schrader's dialogue, filmed with Kathy seated at her desk and the camera following Bill as he circles over her, will bear quoting at length.

BILL: The last three years alone, thirty-five titles, we're talking a cottage industry here. Second only to serial killers – don't get me started – and it's all yours, you get exclusive access: 'Juvenal, as told to Kathy Worthington'.

KATHY (*in a tone of warm, mocking irony*): Aren't you sweet . . . what do you get?

BILL (*very slightly apologetic*): Ninety per cent of everything.

KATHY: That's outrageous.

BILL: That's America. (*He continues without any pause.*) We're talking four, five hundred thou.

KATHY (*Shakes her head, makes a negative noise.*)

BILL: Seventy-five per cent, it's a deal.

The quality I want to note here is again the shared knowledge with which the couple are operating. The point of the key exchange ('That's outrageous'/'That's America') is that if America is outrageous, then these two know it and accept it. The comic collusion set up here reaches its climax in the scene in the KQRD viewing room during Juvenal's TV broadcast, as the events unfolding on screen are accompanied by a kind of family comedy played by Bill, Lynn and Kathy, involving money and doughnuts.

Outrage: Juvenal (Skeet Ulrich) and Lynn (Bridget Fonda) confronting the fanatical August Murray, who tries to murder Lynn, in Paul Schrader's *Touch*. *Source*: British Film Institute.

Outrage is exactly what is absent here. Schrader underlines the point by presenting its opposite in the character of August. He becomes almost an allegorical figure personifying a true form of outrage ('Outrage' is also the name of his organisation), one that defines itself as apart from, not part of, the culture. In this he remains, as they do not, an outsider, one of the 'lonely, self-deluded, sexually inactive people' in which Schrader has expressed a continuing interest (see Jackson, 1990, p.140).

It would be possible to present a number of examples from the second half of *Touch* that would further demonstrate how Schrader has adapted the material in order to emphasise and to enjoy its potential as comedy. He shows us a world in which the miraculous is radically transformed at the point at which it appears in the public realm and becomes the property of the con-men and dealers, all of whom he views with a quality of exasperated affection.

I want to move on to looking at the ways in which Tarantino and Schrader position the couples in their films. In both cases these represent reinflections of the source material, and relate to the way in which each director views the possibilities of his America.

Looking at *Jackie Brown*, we must return to the obviously central question of the effect of changing Jackie's race. What this enables Tarantino to do is to suggest, much more forcefully than if the role were filled by a white woman of the same age and history, both the difficulty of starting over and the gravity of the threat of failure. An example is how the fact that Jackie is black implicitly affects the early scene between Jackie, Nicolet and Dargus, when she is taken in for questioning after being arrested at the airport. In some respects the scene is close to the materials of the novel, but through Pam Grier's performance Tarantino is able to suggest, in his repeated shots of Jackie's face, the fragility of her composure and dignity in front of the two white men. The posture of treating Jackie as if her race is not an issue finally breaks down with Dargus' irritated summary of her position: 'If I was a 44-year-old black woman, desperately clinging on to this one shitty little job that I was fortunate enough to get . . .'

Immediately after this, Tarantino underlines Jackie's desperate situation. When drugs are found in her bag, he almost immediately cuts to his next sequence, using the side of a prison bus moving past a doorway as a linking device. We see Jackie's arrival in the receiving room of a gaol. She is one of a procession of nine women, of whom seven are black. On the soundtrack we hear 'ninety-nine years is a long time . . .' (Les Baxter's 'Long Time Woman', sung by Pam Grier).

This moment can be matched against another, not much later, when Max first sees Jackie as he comes to bail her out of gaol. The long shot of her walking towards him is accompanied by a song of romance: 'Why do I keep my mind / On you, all the time / and I don't even know you' (Charles McCormick's 'Natural High', sung by Bloodstone). This could be summed up as suggesting that, for a woman of Jackie's history and colour, the world offers a few, inflexible, possibilities. The messages of these songs represent the worst, and perhaps one of the better, narratives that are likely to happen to her. (Something related to these extremes is expressed in the sequences' lighting and the resulting photography of skin colour. Compare the stark difference in black and white skin tones in the interrogation sequence, with the shooting of the first scenes with Max and Jackie so that she appears only a little darker than he does.)

Obviously there is no point at which Jackie's race is not an issue. It is clearly central to her relation to Ordell, but also forms a crucial element of what is in play when she brings off her coup of taking the half million dollars from under the noses of Nicolet and Dargus. An element that needs to be added to my earlier discussion of this (see pp.82–3) is that here her race, and the assumptions it carries, work to her advantage. The cops might be suspicious, but one of the reasons for accepting Jackie's story at face value is the difficulty of grasping that a 44-year-old, desperate black woman could outwit them.

Does race play a part in the treatment of the couple at the end of the film? I have already noted that in the novel, where both parties are white, what is at stake is that Jackie is the richer and more intelligent of the two, and Leonard goes a long way in his closing lines to imply that Max's hesitation can be overcome. In Tarantino's film it cannot. The couple, despite their attraction to each other, can sense only their difference, cannot believe in their future. Crucially, Max cannot disentangle himself from the habitual, from his quotidian world. Tarantino places a piece of stage business in the couple's final moments: as they kiss, the telephone rings in the bail bond office and Jackie releases Max with the line that defines him, but that also returns him to his world: 'You're running a business, Max.' The pain and cost of the loss to the man is finely presented, in the last close-ups of Max's devastated face before he moves out of the foreground of the shot and out of focus. It is as if he, renouncing Jackie, loses the definition that his part in these events has briefly given him.

To consider this is immediately to be reminded of *True Romance*, and Tarantino's view that the scripted ending there, in which the woman survives but without the man, is the 'better' one, as opposed to the ending of the Tony Scott film. Perhaps there is a feeling here that the conditions of American success can be pushed only so far: that to escape with the money (Alabama in the *True Romance* screenplay, Jackie here) is success, but it is accompanied by the knowledge of failure, that some other elements of a life have not worked out. Of Jackie and Max we might say that they carry the knowledge of their inability finally to address the larger prejudices that dog the culture in which they have both lived. This position is, of course, consistent with Tarantino's treatment of their physical response to each other, which implicitly remains in the film at the level of strong attraction rather than the sexual intimacy that the novel spells out.

What of the happy couple in *Touch*, what critique is offered of them? It would appear at first that Schrader simply takes over the terms of Leonard's ending, in which the final miracle, which occurs while Juvenal is being interviewed on the talk show, is shrugged off by the viewing public as an obvious fake, and Juvenal and Lynn are allowed to drive contentedly away into American space. Although the broad outlines of this are retained, Schrader does offer, alongside this upbeat ending, an understanding of the couple's limitations.

He does this by suggesting the immaturity of the lovers, as if the condition of their love is that they must be like children. A number of details contribute to this – the suggestion that they look like brother and sister, that they have grown up together (as Juvenal tells Kathy), and Lynn's childlike delight in Juvenal, caught in her repeated use of the word 'neat' to describe him. There is the suggestion that Juvenal in particular can be fooled like a child, through an episode, which is Schrader's invention, of Juvenal believing in a faked photograph that supposedly shows a compromising image of Lynn and Bill Hill. In this context Schrader reintroduces Elwin and Virginia (who do not appear in the novel other than in the opening scene) as figures who are in effect parental. Virginia comments that anyone can see that the photograph is faked, and offers Juvenal's earlier world as one where behaviour was childlike: 'Honey, didn't they have photos down where you were? What did they do, draw in the dirt?'

A single sequence sums up eloquently much of Schrader's fascination with the energy of the culture and his sense of its limitations, and offers a continuation of the presence of versions of the American West. I am thinking of the passage immediately following the sequence discussed above. Juvenal and Lynn escape from LA by hiding out in Buffalo Bill's, a Western themed resort. (This is an actual location, a leisure complex south of Las Vegas that opened in 1994. A theme park based on the West's most famous occasion of showmanship, it boasted the world's tallest roller coaster in 1996.)

Schrader introduces Buffalo Bill's with a single long shot that includes rows of mobile homes, the theme park structures, what looks like a 'toy' train, and the roller coaster. As the camera pans across this landscape, it follows a truck carrying the stacked, neatly crushed remains of a dozen or so cars. We see Juvenal and Lynn enjoy the roller coaster, and then a conversation follows in their hotel bedroom, a themed space with a 'covered wagon' bed, heart-shaped mirror, and entirely faux-Western decoration and props. No comment is made on it other than by Schrader's camera – except that, as the couple start to chat, Juvenal idly uses the remote control to switch the pioneer log fire on and off.

Consumerism, waste, the West as theme park, history as pastiche. Schrader's point is affectionately satirical, but mostly I think he wants us to see Juvenal and Lynn as infantilised, their hotel room as a playroom consonant with the roller coaster and its like outside, in which they lie dressed but barefoot on the floor.

Tarantino's point is that his couple know too much, that they cannot unlearn their lifetime's knowledge of their culture and its prejudices. Schrader's point seems complementary to it, that his lovers can survive, or can at least be allowed to disappear into America, because they allow themselves to know so little, because their feeling is based in a condition in which they can occupy, for a brief period, the roles of happy children.

Thus the two adaptations successfully allow Schrader and Tarantino to take the material in the directions that interest them. My final way of formulating this would be in terms of their finding heroes, or rather locating the heroism of ordinary figures, as perhaps cinema is often able to do, as casting and performance can allow it to do.

So we enjoy the gallery of (self-)promoters in *Touch*. Schrader elicits our sympathy with their heroic struggles: Bill Hill, of course, but also the minor roles: Lolita Davidovitch as Antoinette Baker, the mother of a healed child, Paul Mazursky as Artie, Lynn's old boss (Mazursky is the director of *An Unmarried Woman* and *Down and Out in Beverley Hills* – Schrader's use of him here nicely implies that he knows that film directors can easily be seen as hucksters), Gina Gershon as Debra Lusanne (a change of gender and a much warmer figure than in the Leonard, where the equivalent is more negatively treated), Janeane Garofalo as Kathy. Alongside this has to be put the performance of Bridget Fonda, nicely manoeuvring between the role and life that she knows (witty, cynical young record promoter) and the gift that she can hardly believe that she has been given (to have a genuine adventure of love). All of which begins to sound like talking about *Groundhog Day* – the connection, of course, is being given a gift that you might not be all that sure about at first.

Tarantino takes a genre story about the defeat of a dangerous villain, and while leaving the central structure of the plot alone, embodies his heroes in figures that we do not expect and could not predict from, say, a reading of *Rum Punch*. A great deal here turns on casting, and *Jackie Brown* is the exemplary case of Tarantino's extraordinary sureness of touch in this area. The heroine and hero, as embodied by Pam Grier and Robert Foster, are of course highly unusual castings for these slots. The fact that neither Grier nor

Foster are substantial box office stars crucially affects what they present. We see black, no longer quite young, womanhood and late middle age in the man, in a context in which it lacks the safety net of being embodied in a major star. (Late middle age in, say, a Jack Nicholson part is an example of the safety net.)

In their strangeness, Grier and Foster inevitably invite us to fill in the outline by invoking the past – we turn to their film histories. Or perhaps to a general sense that they *have* histories, ones that we cannot recall just at the moment, but that act in the cinema to create a feeling of depth, of pasts. Tarantino's famously encyclopedic recall goes along with an awareness that we do not have to know what he knows, that we can infer the sense of a past without having to specify it in detail.

The success of the casting is emphasised by the use in other roles in the film of those who might be unsurprising in leading roles. No preconceptions regarding stars would be disturbed by another movie we can invent for a moment, with Bridget Fonda as a white Jackie, Robert De Niro as Max Cherry, Pam Grier as one of Ordell's older, doomed girlfriends, and Robert Foster as a sad ex-convict: *Rum Punch* as it might conventionally have been cast and filmed.

7 *Kill Bill*: excursion into style

> The film was, of course, a relentless excursion into style, which, taken for granted in any work of art, is considered to be unpardonable in this medium.
>
> (Josef von Sternberg (1965), writing on *The Scarlet Empress* in his autobiography *Fun in a Chinese Laundry*)

The fourth film by Quentin Tarantino

I want to take up an invitation offered in the opening credits of *Kill Bill Vol.1*, one carried in a statement that was part of its pre-release publicity and that is offered here as a declaration: 'The 4th Film by Quentin Tarantino'. In a film industry in which sequels and series are now so common, this title might be thought knowingly to pose both a reassurance (those who have enjoyed the previous three can hope that they know what they will be getting) and a challenge (exactly how is this film like and unlike the others?). It also prompts a question about the division of *Kill Bill* into its two volumes. Are these one film (on a future DVD, perhaps) or two (as we experience them in the cinema, separated by some months in release date)? Is *Vol.2* the fifth film by Quentin Tarantino? Whatever else may be the case, what is certainly being insisted on is the importance of the director and the connection with earlier work. The invitation is to compare this film (these films) to the previous three. (In discussing the films I shall refer to *Kill Bill* when thinking of both together, and *Vol.1* and *Vol.2* when taking them separately.)

One of the most productive ways to compare *Kill Bill* to the first three films is to think about geographical location, not simply where the films are set but also the treatment of the places. It is at once evident that the earlier films are set in a familiar or ordinary America – ordinary, that is, to the characters who populate it, and also to us. We are offered different locales in American cities – mostly in the single megalopolis of LA. Tarantino's liking for introducing locations by written titles is a part of this insistence on their availability, say their visitability: we believe that we could travel to them if we wished. The familiarity is sometimes underlined by the invocation of the rest of the globe as strange, evidently extraordinary to those who think of themselves as at home. *Reservoir Dogs* deals almost entirely with a few spots in a single city, with a few decorative details (the globe and map in the set of Joe Cabot's office) recalling an idea of other continents. *Pulp Fiction* acknowledges, as I have argued, the existence of Europe as a way of expressing the reach of Marcellus' empire, but it is a world that exists in the film mainly in the recollection of its oddities, what a quarter-pounder is called in France. In *Jackie Brown* Spain is invoked for its exotic quality, a place threateningly unlike the known world to someone like Max Cherry. Mexico is at the other end of the airline route, and the telephone line, but we never go there.

Kill Bill treats some of its locations quite differently. This is not just a matter of dimension, the reach to China or Japan or Mexico. Although that is clearly a difference, it is less important than the ways that the places are constructed and invoked. They broadly fall into two types. One follows the first three films and is ordinary or visitable places: a suburban street in Pasadena, a wedding chapel outside El Paso, a small bar in Okinawa, a mobile home set down in a remote spot in California, and a strip joint in a town nearby.

Counterpointing these are other worlds, or settings, that are evidently of a different kind. One way of recognising this is that it is not at all clear how you might travel to them, what form of transport or state of mind the journey might require. Examples are the home of Pai Mei, the snow garden behind the Blue Leaves restaurant, and the attic of the Okinawa bar (if that is what it is: its geographical connection with the bar is not quite clear) that houses the collection of Hanzo swords. We might characterise these as places that someone on a quest might need to visit, but where they might not be required, or would not wish, to stay for longer than necessary.

Outside Tarantino's work this distinction is, of course, familiar. A straightforward case of it is the difference between Kansas and the Land of Oz in *The Wizard of Oz*. In Tarantino's case the distinctions are slippery: for example, having to account for locations that are apparently mundane (say, a restaurant or a home) but that briefly seem to be taken over as sites for a ritual, or a battle, and then presumably are allowed to return to the ordinary world again.

A way of marking the distinction that I am pondering here would be to consider the actual or potential function of money in these different settings. In all the previous films we could say that money, and the consciousness of the importance of possessing greater or lesser amounts of it, are central to everyone (as it is in the world of Dorothy's Kansas). In those parts of *Kill Bill* in which the ordinary world has fallen away, so has ordinary money, which can have no function or meaning in, say, Pai Mei's home, or in the Snow Garden (any more than it does in the Land of Oz). The moments that express characters' relations to ordinary sums of money and the transactions associated with them in the first three films, the kinds of considerations that make Mr Pink reluctant to tip, or Ordell proud of owning a house, do not apply in these worlds. But we can imagine money changing hands in the ordinary worlds with which *Kill Bill* also works: in, say, the wedding chapel, or the My-Oh-My bar.

The City of Pasadena, California

I now want to turn to *Vol.1*, where we can see how some of these issues are laid out for us in the opening minutes. Tarantino begins with a couple of devices that remind us that we are dealing with a medium that is subject to technical considerations and that, either by a show of eerie perfection or by their evident imperfection, remind us of past and present technologies, of cinema's history. The fuzzy sound and wobbly image of the Shawscope and 'Our Feature Presentation' screens are followed a little later by the opposite mode. This is exemplified by the high quality of modern sound reproduction, here the perfect clarity of Nancy Sinatra's performance of 'Bang Bang' (appropriately chosen, because so precisely enunciated by the singer, every consonant present) played over the credits. What this promises is that we are going to be offered a film that will foreground cinematic techniques, both new ones and some that have a past.

Between these two devices is the film's prologue, the blood-spattered bride (whose name we learn much later is Beatrix Kiddo (Uma Thurman)) panting as she lies on the floor of the wedding chapel, listening to Bill's (David Carradine) speech. We are shown plausible terror, a concentration on the image of one body for which pain and imminent death are apparently not avoidable, with the qualities of realism that can be carried by black-and-white photography. The presence of quotidian reality is delivered by a simple gesture (here, wiping the blood off a face with a folded handkerchief while making a speech, which might remind us of an analogous gesture, Larry's care for Freddy in *Reservoir Dogs*).

The shift from the realism of this scene to one that can be treated in quite another mode occurs as the main narrative gets under way. We have a familiar kind of establishing shot. It is an unexceptional bourgeois American home, squarely framed with off-centre trees and lawn running down to the pavement. The accompanying written title (a device of which, as I

have said previously, Tarantino is fond and which he always uses strategic-
ally) reads: 'The City of Pasadena, California'. A real place. As we watch
this image, the truck driven by Beatrix draws up. But she now looks, not
towards the house that we have seen, but in the other direction, towards the
camera. She is looking at the house on the opposite side of the street.

We cut to that house, and the contrast is instructive. The house is small,
with bright-green clapboards, and is a bungalow (at least it appears to have
no upper windows) with a steeply gabled roof and porch – it looks, not like
the well-established building on the other side of the street, but like a doll's
house, or a house from a movie or stage set, having an affinity with the toys
distributed on the lawn in front of it. So we are being nudged towards a
world that partakes both of the real (this could still just be a plausible
house in a California suburb) and the fantastic (this is a doll's house, a
toy house).

Moments later two women, Beatrix and Vernita Green (Vivica A. Fox),
meet and instantly fight. Elements of the way the fight is presented are
pursued in some of the later combats in *Kill Bill*: a physical encounter
between bodies that is an occasion for an exploration of cinematic effects.
We see the intricate editing and the association of each movement with a
cue on the soundtrack: even a body moving through the air is given an
audible sound effect. The concentration is not on the effectiveness or
otherwise of any given blow; there is no sense of progressive victory by one
party over another. The point of view is not significantly that of either
woman once the fight begins, and what interest there is in victory or defeat
is not presented as a narrative. The convention is that this combat is
an engagement of apparent equals that will be suddenly ended by a fatal
stroke, not a gradual vanquishing. It could be compared to a dance that
ends when one partner suddenly flees, or sinks to the ground.

In Chapter 3 I suggested that there is an important distinction to be made
between this and another mode of violence, which is an exercise of power
by one party over another. This latter mode wrenches us through our
awareness of helplessness and our anticipation of seeing power exercised:
the ear-cutting in *Reservoir Dogs* and Bill leaning over the prone bride in
Vol.1 are examples of it. In much of *Kill Bill* the violence is presented with
no such structure of power and anticipation. The fight here is an excuse for
noting exact aesthetic effects (which those fighting cannot know and would
not care about), such as the tinkling sound of glass underfoot, and for
enjoying the spectacle of destruction (again, glass is important) that never
seriously harms those who collide with the objects.

This dance of violence can be the occasion for a celebration of the
elegance of the choreography and the techniques with which such a
sequence can be photographed. Two examples: one is the moment when

Vernita's daughter Nikki (Ambrosia Kelley) appears, the shot taken through the picture window framed by the two combatant women either side of it: Nikki steps off the school bus perfectly into the dead centre of the frame, the grid of the window glazing serving to emphasise this, as if it were a sectioned drawing. The other is the shots taken from directly overhead as the two women pause after their first fight, and again as Beatrix retrieves her knife from Vernita's body.

This chapter ends with a reversal of its opening, an expression of a return to the other world. We see Beatrix, her face now a little blood-spattered but otherwise unmarked, seated again in her truck, from the same point of view as the first shot of her: the Pasadena home from the title shot is in the background. Then she drives away, through a wide, generously lawned street that is entirely familiar, a definitive image of American suburbia.

What I want to take away from this is the idea that Tarantino begins his film by suggesting to us that there is a world that conforms to familiar rules, in which you might lie beaten up on a wooden floor, be shot dead by a lover, in which violence is progressively painful. There is also a world, let us call it an extraordinary world, in which you might spring up effectively unharmed from blows inflicted on you, and in which an impulse to kill for vengeance might be enactable and might seem right. But these two worlds can easily become confused. I take it that it is to emphasise and explore this last point that Tarantino includes the little girl in the sequence. She produces a nice confusion between what is due to the ordinary (cereal when a small child comes home from school, politeness to one's mother's visitors) and what Beatrix wants of this encounter, a fantasy of getting at least a little bit even.

Issues of order and shape

How are these subjects projected into the film, or films, as a whole? To answer this I want to look at the tricky question of structure, of the order of events. Again Tarantino seems to foreground this, to invite consideration of it, at the very beginning of the film, not only by numbering the main characters (Uma Thurman's apart) in the order on which they will appear on Beatrix's death list (which we see is called 'Death List One', as if everything were part of some series or other) but also opening the Vernita Green sequence with a title that calls it 'Chapter One' followed by a hand-circled numeral two. Tarantino is emphasising that what we are seeing is out of order, that he has (characteristically) taken the elements of his story and rearranged them. But as the films proceed we inevitably engage in a reconstruction, making sense by achieving at least an approximate idea of the narrative in the order in which the events must have occurred. I want to consider what we find when we do this, which is something like this:

1. We are in a schoolroom, where a small child named Beatrix Kiddo answers her name at roll-call. But the image of that child is not directly available. Occupying the seat is not the child but the figure of the adult that she will become.
2. At around the same time, another small child (Oren Ishii) watches her parents die at the hands of gangsters. Two years later, she is ('luckily for her', in the words of the narrating voice) offered to their murderer as a child to be sexually abused. She avenges her parents' deaths by killing the murderer, and embarks on a career as an assassin. Again there is something unusual about our access to this story, in that it is shown in Japamation (and told in voice-over).
3. It is something like 15 or 20 years later than (1), and we are somewhere in China. This sequence is filmed without cartoon or other stylisation. A story is told about a teacher and revenge for bad manners. Beatrix, shown as a very young woman – a ponytail and a backpack, and later on even pigtails – is being sent off by a man who looks fatherly (Bill). She is to receive instruction from another patriarch, Pai Mei (Gordon Liu), in the martial arts, and other forms of addressing the power of life and death over others.
4. Beatrix survives the cruel tutelage of Pai Mei and, along with whatever knowledge she has acquired from Bill, becomes highly adept at taking life.
5. Oren Ishii, now played by Lucy Liu, becomes the 'queen of the Tokyo underworld' and similarly highly skilled in killing people.
6. Beatrix and Oren are by now part of a group – the Deadly Viper Assassination Squad – that is led by Bill and includes his brother Buddy (Michael Madsen) and two other women, one of whom at least has been tutored by Pai Mei. Although we understand that they exist in a world apart we see nothing of it, and nothing that is to do with the lives they take.
7. Beatrix and Bill are lovers, although we do not see anything of this. Beatrix finds that she is pregnant by Bill. She decides to abandon her current life and seek another world for her unborn daughter. Her first step in doing this is to explain it to another woman, an assassin from a rival organisation, sent to kill her.
8. Beatrix disappears, takes an ordinary job. Seven or so months later she is about to be married to a complaisant, simple man. She has been tracked down by Bill and he and the other members of the Deadly Vipers massacre the wedding party, leaving Beatrix for dead.

A young woman about to place herself under the tutelage of a patriarch: Beatrix (Uma Thurman) at the foot of Pai Mei's steps in *Kill Bill Vol.2*. *Source*: British Film Institute.

9. Beatrix is not dead, but in a coma from a shot in the head. Her child is delivered and somehow acquired by Bill. He considers having Beatrix killed by lethal injection, but aborts this action at the very last minute.

10. Four years pass. Beatrix, waking from her coma, is reborn into the world. She knows nothing of her daughter, and seems to assume that the child died. She travels to the East again, this time to Okinawa. She pretends to be a young tourist, a little like the figure of her earlier self, the girl who was accepted as a pupil by Pai Mei. She persuades another patriarch, Hattori Hanzo (Sonny Chiba), to accept her and to make her a sword with which to kill her enemies. He will do this for some unexplained reason that causes him to wish to see Bill dead.

11. Beatrix travels to Tokyo, fights and kills Oren Ishii (who is still queen of that underworld) and her bodyguards, with the sword that Hanzo has made.

12. She returns to America and confronts another of the Deadly Vipers who has left the life: Vernita Green, who is now a mother in Pasadena. She fights and kills her.

13. She travels to a remote spot in California where Buddy lives in partial retreat from the world. She tries to kill him but the man with the shotgun overcomes the woman with the sword. He proposes to kill her slowly by burying her alive. Using the skills acquired from Pai Mei she escapes from her lonely grave and returns but Buddy is already dead, executed by one of the other assassins, Elle Driver (Daryl Hannah), evidently in revenge for an old enmity that is never explained. She fights and defeats Elle, leaving her blind.

14. She leaves for Mexico to confront Bill. Arriving at his hacienda she discovers that her daughter is living, and has been brought up by Bill, although she knows that Beatrix is her mother. She kills Bill, and rides off with her daughter.

15. The film reaches its chronological end, the mother and daughter in a motel room watching cartoons on TV, surely an image of the ordinariness of this family relation.

To lay the narrative out in this way makes a number of aspects of it clearer.

We see not only how substantially Tarantino has reordered the events but also how they have been distributed across the two halves of the film. (Roughly *Vol.1* includes numbers 2, 5, 6, 9, 10, 11 and 12 of the sections laid out above, and *Vol.2* offers 1, 3, 4, 7, 8, 13, 14 and 15.) In both cases the narrative structure is carefully organised to avoid confusing the viewer too much: we are assisted by a core of chronological material interrupted by events out of sequence: *Vol.1* has a chronological core of 6, 9, 10 and 11 interrupted by 2, 5 and 12, and *Vol.2* offers 8, 13, 14 and 15 interrupted by 1, 3, 4 and 7.

More significantly, we can see that the reordered story falls into two parallel parts. The break point is the ritual death and rebirth of the figure: the wedding chapel massacre and the revival from the coma. That this is a pivotal event of the films is emphasised by both of them using it in their openings. The parallels between the two parts can be plotted clearly if we adopt for a moment the convention of calling the first figure Beatrix and the second (revived) one the Bride, whereupon we find the following.

In both cases the starting point is a woman who looks (or chooses to act) like a young girl and who is placed, or places herself, in an intense relationship to older, patriarchal figures (Beatrix to Bill and Pai Mei, the Bride to Hattori Hanzo). In both cases she becomes a killer (Beatrix's victims are those targeted by the Deadly Vipers: the Bride's victims are the remaining members of the Deadly Vipers). She is overcome in the middle of this killing by knowledge that has to do with her child (for Beatrix the knowledge that she is pregnant, for the Bride the knowledge that her daughter is alive). In both cases this knowledge results in events that take her away from Bill and towards the ordinary world (for Beatrix the state of marriage after she has fled from Bill, for the Bride the state of motherhood after she has killed Bill).

What can be grasped from this is how much the materials of *Kill Bill* suggest a film about the choice of departure from the ordinary world and the desire to return to it: in its two parts it enacts a repetition of that trajectory. The worlds that define the journeys can be laid out thus:

1. A world in which you understand (or construct) yourself to be a young person with things to learn, in which you put yourself in the relation of educated to instructor, or even disciple to master.
2. A world in which you exercise extraordinary powers, one in which you are a member of something with a title, like the Deadly Viper Assassination Squad, or otherwise marked as possibly invincible.
3. A domestic world to which you return (at the cost of losing these powers?), in which you choose to assume a role in a family, but now as mother, rather than as daughter. But how well you are suited for this role is in question.

I am conscious of the dangers of discussing a film Tarantino chose not to make. So I now want to take this analysis back to the events in the order in which Tarantino has caused us to experience them, and by doing so produced two films that are, I shall argue, radically different in tone and meaning.

Vol.1: Success – the American girl goes east

It should be clear by now that the Pasadena sequence of *Vol.1* serves as something that we could think of as an overture to the narrative, laying out Beatrix's two impulses. To sum up, they are the desire to get even (to make the world one of extraordinary violence that works in your favour) and the need to acknowledge an ordinary world (one that includes daughters and mothers, Nikki's world) to which you might wish eventually to return.

After Pasadena, Tarantino takes us back to the ruined bride in the wedding chapel, and then to the hospital in which Beatrix awakes from her coma. The consistent note in these scenes has to do with the forms of relation of her prone body to men, and specifically to the penetration of that body. I am thinking of her killing of the man who violated her while she was unconscious, Buck (Michael Bowen), and the man who wished to do so, credited only as 'the trucker' (Johnathan Loughran). There is also her spitting in the face of the sheriff and the typically witty condensation of the motif into an image of the four-year sleep broken by the sensation of being probed by a passing mosquito, as if rage at this prick is what kicks Beatrix back into life. (Added to the list should be penetration by agent, the needleful of poison that Bill sends Elle Driver to inject into Beatrix's bloodstream.) We could notice that Tarantino chooses not to show us exactly how the trucker dies, as if Beatrix's sheer rage is enough to kill him.

The next extended narrative of the film is the history of Oren Ishii, told in the Japamation sequence that recounts the story of her witnessing the death of her parents as a child and the child's revenge on their murderer two years later. The question that presses on us immediately is: why is this story told this way, as animation rather than live action?

One clue is provided by the context. The tale is told by Beatrix, while she lies in the back of Buck's truck attempting to will her comatose legs back into action. It is framed by two shots in which she addresses her big toe, first attempting to will it into movement, and finally succeeding in doing so. Her imagination moves from what she remembers about the Deadly Vipers (four faces looking down at her prone body) to what she knows about Oren, and the Japamation is perhaps a way of expressing how Beatrix imagines, or wants to present to us, someone else's story of violence and revenge. The Japamation presents the juxtaposition of absolute innocence and equally absolute villainy, and offers an access to the effects of violence that is free of the corporeal and its limitations (so, absolute rainfalls and showers of blood, as much blood as will satisfy the desire for revenge rather than just the amount that might leak messily from a body). It allows freedom from the constraints of space (as when Oren, having killed Boss Masumoto, vanishes into thin air). The sense that an ideal scenario is being played out for us is greatly underlined by the use of the score's richest and most sonorous melody, Luis Bacalov's 'The Grand Duel', as the soundtrack music here. It is also the case that in this imagined world we can be offered, and deal with, images that would be overwhelmingly vicious if presented in live action (the mother's blood dripping on to the face of the 9-year-old Oren as she lies under the bed) or simply impossible within the conventions of censorship (the 11-year-old Oren astride the body of the paedophile Yakuza boss as she kills him).

That the animation has as much to do with the consciousness of the teller as it does with what is told is made clear by the last moves of the sequence. As we move from the child to the adult Oren, Tarantino does not use the convenience of this ellipsis to cut back to live action, and even presents the bride's final brief recollection of the massacre at the wedding chapel in the same mode.

This is the first part of the history of Oren. In the second part of it Beatrix transfers some of the terms of the Japamation sequence to the live-action world. The introduction to Oren's position as queen of the underworld, and to her defenders, uses freeze-frame, and blood presented as floods or geysers, some of the terms of the Japamation. (These are also to be found in the Japanese revenge movie of the 1970s, of which *Lady Snowblood* (Toshiya Fujita, 1973) has been the example widely promoted as an influence on Tarantino.)

These passages of historical background are ones in which Beatrix cannot possibly appear (Oren's childhood) or cannot yet appear (the introduction of the Tokyo underworld). They are nonetheless possessed by her and communicated to us through her, via her almost continuously present voice-over and the Japamation. We should bear in mind that these are the *only* extended passages of *Kill Bill* in which Beatrix is not either present or about to make an entrance (as she is, for example, in Buddy's world in *Vol.2*, which is not characterised through voice-over). The effect is to insist on the complete domination of the film by the central role. Even when Beatrix is not physically present, the events described are told largely through her voice and seen in her mind's eye.

The next moves of the film, the preparations (by which I mean both the Bride's preparations and the way the film is preparing us) for the show-down at the Blue Leaves restaurant, involve a familiar proposition – that if a revenger is to win against impossible odds, then what must be invoked is a kind of magic, and particularly a weapon that is so undefeatable that it could be thought of as enchanted. Such a weapon can be represented in a number of ways. Here the emphasis is not mainly on the mystical or sacramental elements, but includes an appropriately American stress on unsurpassable quality of manufacture – not only a Hattori Hanzo sword but the best sword he has made, by his own account.

Alongside this, Tarantino prepares us with a series of distinctions between the two sides. On the one hand, Okinawa is associated with measure, tradition/craft, a ceremonial of white robes suggestive of a near priesthood, a withdrawal from the world and its violence and crucially with celibacy (the odd couple that is Hanzo and his bald sidekick, set up in the comedy of their opening scene). Compare this with Tokyo: black robes, power brokered by enforcers (the Crazy 88) and lawyers (Sophie Fatale

(Julie Dreyfus)). The gangster's council is wittily shown as a parodic form of modern despotism in the sequence following Oren's beheading of Boss Tanaka (Jun Kunimura), in which her speech in English to the council is reproduced in simultaneous translation by Sophie as it rises to a screaming rant.

Perhaps the most telling comparison is in the positioning of the image of a young woman, and the relations she chooses to assume with men. In Okinawa we have the Bride's 'young tourist' act with Hanzo when she arrives at the bar, as if she understands that she must first assume the position of an unthreatening good daughter before revealing her mission. (She is recycling her relation to Pai Mei, but we do not know this until *Vol.2.*) The parallel figure in Tokyo is Gogo Yubari (Chiaki Kuriyama), Oren's bodyguard, whose dress as a 'Japanese schoolgirl' specifically references pornographic images of the sexually available child, and whose introductory character note is one of sexual violence: the scene in which she makes a sexual invitation and then stabs the man to death.

I regret not having space to discuss the sequence of the fight in the Blue Leaves restaurant at length. It can be thought of as a climax to that side of the film that celebrates the heroine's journey, her arrival in a world in which her powers are supreme. The shape of what we see is generically familiar: the heroine will defeat not only implausible numbers of ordinary antagonists (the Crazy 88), but also the more potent figures who, we can enjoy thinking for a moment, might almost conquer her: the psychopathic sidekick, Gogo, and finally the single villainous antagonist, Oren. The sequence reprises elements of the Pasadena fight with Vernita but without the clash between the quotidian world and the extraordinary one. Here those who are not fighters make a speedy exit from the scene and the troubling child is alluded to but quickly converted into comedy (the little boy who is spanked and sent home by Beatrix for playing with Yakusas).

Tarantino's celebration of all this is to take it as an occasion of the relentless assertion of techniques: black-and-white photography, distortions in the ways in which intervals of time pass for the combatants, even most startlingly the moment in which the players fight in silhouette against a blue matte screen sectioned into squares, a moment of reference to the medium that seems designed to force us (if nothing else so far has managed it) to feel the freedom from constraint, the escape into a world still more enchanted, still more remote. (A shift into dream sequence in a musical comes to mind as making an analogous leap.)

Finally, the sequence is used to offer an intense concentration on the human face as well as the athletic body. The photography of the fights between the protagonist and a single antagonist – Gogo and Beatrix, Oren and Beatrix – are examples of how important and marked this interest is.

A world in which her powers are supreme: the Bride (Uma Thurman) in the showdown at the Blue Leaves restaurant in *Kill Bill Vol.1*. *Source*: British Film Institute.

On this note of intense energy and achievement, *Vol.1* comes to an end, a little like a musical that ends with a massively satisfying number.

Vol.2: Failure – the American girl and the New West

One way in which the two *Kill Bill* films can be contrasted is in the shape of the journeys they portray. *Vol.1* effectively records Beatrix's movement from America to Japan (the effect of showing the Vernita and Oren killings in reverse chronological order being to reinforce this impression). *Vol.2* is solidly set in America, in El Paso and then California (with the single extended flashback to China), and then follows the road south, resembling in this a number of famous American narratives, to end across the border in Mexico. For the viewer of *Vol.1*, *Vol.2* is also presented explicitly as a return to America from Japan: after the prologue at the wedding chapel, a short sequence between Bill and Buddy sketching the events at the Blue Leaves restaurant establishes this.

There are other ways in which *Vol.2* presents itself early as a film about America. Consider the much extended reprise of the El Paso wedding chapel massacre, which is the film's first episode. The images here are of a familiar cinematic West: the isolation of the chapel, the use of black-and-white photography, the interest in weather-beaten and worn surfaces (the cracked paintwork on the porch of the chapel, the scoured boards on which Bill and Beatrix stand, every contour in their grain showing in the image), the choice of soundtrack music. That the location is chosen for its expressiveness is hinted at by the fact that no reason is given for the Bride wanting to marry her record-store-owning groom in such a relatively remote place. The people with whom Tarantino fills the scene are a mixture of the traditional and the modern West. The innocent and effusive Tommy (Christopher Allan Nelson) and the three young girls are all presumably from the city, but there are also stock Western figures: the Reverend (Bo Svenson) and his good wife and the piano player with his history of those who have passed through, and passed on. All these elements create an image of a place at once homely and lonely, in which pieties are spread thin across empty land. The stress is on the difficulty of sustaining life, especially family life. In terms of movement, the sequence references those Westerns that have made so much of the doorway and porch, and the image of a single woman hesitating at a threshold.

Such lives were in the Western always threatened by violence, and violence in the different form of the Deadly Vipers destroys them here. (It is typical of Tarantino's strategic direction of violence that this brutal exercise of power against the innocent is something that he does not show us, the camera remaining firmly outside the chapel as the wedding party die.)

Tarantino then takes us from a version of the fragility of the civilisation of the West to a version of its degeneration. After an establishing shot of arid country we now find the modern Westerner. What is placed in this wilderness is not a pioneer in a log cabin, but Buddy sitting and drinking in the doorway of his shabby mobile home, surrounded by miscellaneous debris. (Suggestively, Tarantino does not identify this place with a written title, as if it is nowhere that is usually written down.) The following sequence extends and explores this version of Western vacancy: the My-Oh-My bar, where Buddy works as a bouncer, with its empty car park and deserted interior, is a location in which Tarantino characterises the clash between the habits of urban culture and this declined West. Larry (Larry Bishop), the boss of the joint, sits in his poky, cluttered office with one of the girls, his desk covered in drugs and money, unable to bear the fact that Buddy's excuse for his lateness is that the place is deserted anyway, and particularly enraged by one celebrative gesture, Buddy's concession to the dandyness of the Westerner, which is the immaculate cowboy hat he wears to work. The mood is capped by a final image, of pollution. Another one of the girls tells Buddy that the toilets are overflowing and it is his job to clean it up.

So if this version of the new West is so much drugs and shit, then ought not Buddy to be an easy target for the heroine who disposed of the Crazy 88? Beatrix charges the door of the trailer, intent on killing Buddy with a sword thrust, only to be blasted off her feet by the force of a shotgun loaded with rock salt, and to have the Hanzo sword kicked contemptuously into the distance as Buddy stands over her prone body.

The trope is a familiar one in American culture, essentially an argument between two kinds of hunter: the figure with the scattergun, or shotgun, or cannon, and the figure who kills with one blow, typically a perfectly aimed spear, or deadly accurate rifle. (It can be traced back, to pick two well-known instances, to the pigeon-shooting episode in James Fenimore Cooper's *The Pioneers* (1823), or, say, to Howard Hawks *El Dorado* (1967)). The point is not that one or other of these modes is the correct one, but that each is capable of defeating the other. There is also an idea of technological development here: the best samurai sword in the world is easily defeated by a man using a firearm that requires only average skill (as if Beatrix were an Indian with a bow and arrow). It is worth noting here that the Hanzo sword, so deadly in Tokyo, is used in America, but never to fatal effect. To underline Beatrix's defeat, Tarantino repeats a motif from *Vol.1*, the pricking of her body with needles: Buddy casually pumps an injection of sedative into her.

The episode of 'The Lonely Grave of Paula Schultz', and its flashback to the Bride's tutelage by Pai Mei, offers in Eastern guise something that is very familiar as a subject in Westerns – the importance of teaching and learning, and thus of self-reliance. As is commonly the case, the learning process is not offered as a very congenial one, nor is the teacher a necessarily congenial figure (Pai Mei is an almost parodic dandy). What this emphasises is that what is important is not the particular qualities of the tutor or the tutee, but the fact that knowledge can be transmitted, and specifically across generations, from an old-timer (Pai Mei is certainly that) to a neophyte. In Westerns, very commonly what is at stake is either knowledge of how to kill, or how to save yourself – images of the absolute importance of knowing things.

Tarantino invests this episode with cinematic bravura, taking us into the coffin with Beatrix and finding a way of involving us, through those passages in which our eyes interrogate a black or nearly black screen for signs of life or movement, with the completeness of her loneliness and the absoluteness of the self-reliance she is now called upon to show. The culminating moment of the flashback is the image of her ravaged hands picking up rice with chopsticks. This gives way to the series of actions that end with her punching her way through the coffin, images of exercising control of the world through control of the body in circumstances in which you are, or feel, entirely alone. (The sequence can be related back to another image of calling on the body to perform in *Vol.1*, the prone figure in the back of her truck willing her big toe to move.)

The final image of the West that I wish to consider involves looking at two sequences, the death of Buddy, poisoned by snakebite from the black mamba that Elle has concealed in the money she brings to him, and the fight between Elle and Beatrix. In the first of these it is a collection of details that particularly interest me.

1. The pornographic magazines that fall in a scatter on the floor as Buddy writhes in his death agony.
2. The strangely old-fashioned holder for memos and letters that is on the wall of the trailer behind Buddy's head in some of these shots.
3. Elle's notebook, from which she reads out information (that she tells us is taken from the Internet) on the deadliness of the black mamba's poison.

I suggest that these details are highly strategic, expressive of the incoherent nature of Buddy's West. They invoke both the West that we still associate with American pieties and ideals, the world in which writings were once neatly filed under categories (the memo/letter holder), the fallen, modern world of mechanical reproductions (the pornography) and the postmodern world of information systems (the notes from the Net). Buddy's destiny is to die while what is being read over him is not the Good Book, but the result of an Internet search.

This incoherence can be connected with the presentation of the fight between Elle and Beatrix, the last extended swordfight in the film. If we compare it to the fight with Vernita in *Vol.1*, a number of interesting issues arise. It is clearly similar in a number of respects – an excuse for bravura (both stunting and camerawork), a similar kind of combat where blows do not disable and there is no gradual narrative of victory and defeat, but a sudden ending with a single blow. But to look at the two together is to be struck with the degree to which the latter is about fighting in a rubbish pit. The trailer is both full of junk and is itself junk, falling to pieces as the two women smash about in it. The moment in which Beatrix throws some kind of sticky substance (jam?) into Elle's face (it elicits the comment 'Gross!' from Elle, which gets a laugh from the audience) only underlines the point about mess, as does the washing-off of the same muck when Beatrix tries to drown Elle in the trailer's toilet bowl. There is nothing remotely comparable to these moments in the fight with Vernita, and of course the sharpest contrast is reserved for the ending, the fact that Beatrix does not deliver a mortal blow to Elle, but disables her by putting out her remaining eye, leaving her blindly thrashing around in the disgusting ruins of the trailer. The squalid scene is also in explicit contrast to the elegance of the snow garden in *Vol.1*, of which Oren was moved to say to Beatrix that 'as last looks go, you could do worse'.

If we take stock at this point it is startling to realise the sharpness of the contrast with *Vol.1*. There the association of killing is predominantly with revenge that seemed justified to the revenger, or with the destruction of

Squalor: Elle Driver (Darryl Hannah) squares up for her combat with the Bride in the confines of Buddy's trailer in *Kill Bill Vol.2*. *Source*: British Film Institute.

monsters (Vernita, Buck and the trucker, Oren's killing of Boss Masumoto, the Crazy 88, Gogo, Oren). Here it is replaced with vengeance of a different kind: within the film's present time there are Buddy's death agonies and the horror of leaving Elle flailing in the rubbish. In the flashbacks we have the massacre of the innocent bridal party and the poisoning of Pai Mei. In every case the moments invoke a feeling of sneakiness or the stealthy. The two cases of poisoning are clear enough – this was always connected with the underhand – but I would also include the attack on the eye in the middle of a swordfight in this category.

What is shown to falter in *Vol.2* is the sense of the rightness or authority of Beatrix's mission. In fact, she has killed nobody in the course of this film at this point (and will kill nobody apart from Bill). The West, even in its degeneration (or perhaps particularly in this state) does not offer the satisfactions provided by Tokyo, or even Pasadena, but rather the view that all these figures are equally guilty. Towards the opening of the film, Buddy – its dissolute but still perhaps its representative Westerner – makes a declarative statement of this position, which we can see now as quite different from that of *Vol.1*: 'That woman deserves her revenge, and we deserve to die . . . then again, so does she.'

Mexico: the end of the road

This brings me to the final movement of *Vol.2*, which begins with Beatrix crossing into Mexico, and ends with her departure with her daughter B.B. after killing Bill. The first important issue here is the crossing of a border. Tarantino is using a familiar literary and filmic trope in which the image of the sexually available Mexican woman is at the centre of the contrast between Mexico and the United States, with the implication that over the border sexual activity is less regulated by law but often more subject to the control exercised by a father figure. In different cases this can be inflected more or less positively, from, say, Angel's utopian village in *The Wild Bunch* (1968) through to the extreme combination of wonder and anarchy in the Mexican brothel sequences that are part of the final journey in Jack Kerouac's novel *On the Road* (1957). Here the presentation is markedly negative: the sinister parental figure of Esteban Vihaio (Michael Parks), formally polite and evidently villainous. The point is underlined in the discussion of punishment, and the due presentation for our (and Beatrix's) brief inspection, of the girl whose mouth Vihaio has slit. This can be connected back to the blinding of Elle: the film is presenting a world in which punishment is no longer death but something arguably more sadistic – mutilation.

The film then seems to move in a new direction. What Beatrix finds when she reaches Bill is not some evidently degenerate world but a family home, admittedly a rich one, in which a father and a daughter are playing a game. Or, the daughter is playing a game: perhaps the father is attempting to convert what Beatrix wants to do – to kill him – into a game, to suggest that she might try thinking of it as one.

My reading of what then happens in the home is this. Bill is a monster, a kind of ogre, alone in the home with his fairy-tale daughter (the adjective being what the casting and presentation of Perla Haney-Jardine seems intended to suggest). He is also a good parent, making sandwiches, explaining the difference between right and wrong, pointing out that *Shogun Assassin* is too long for the filmic equivalent of a bedtime story. His object in these scenes, apart from showing off his good parenthood, seems to be entirely clear, which is to convince Beatrix that she is like him – that is, an ogress – or, as he calls it, a 'natural born killer', a 'renegade killer bee'. He does this by proposing it directly to her, which is the point of his little lecture on Superman. In addition, with the aid of the truth serum (the last of the darts and needles that Beatrix is to be subjected to), he attempts to make her confess it to him and, more importantly, to herself.

She does so, but the result is a kind of deadlock, a family that cannot possibly be made right: they cannot agree to be monsters together. (Possibly, as Beatrix argues, this is because she at least imagines something else for her daughter, even though she may not be able to give it to her.) So one of them must kill the other, or they must kill each other. At this very late stage Bill seems to recognise the sadness of all this and responds by getting a little drunk.

Beatrix kills Bill by using the exploding heart technique. It is yet another piece of magic with the hands that Pai Mei has taught her, and needs to be put in some contexts that I have raised already. It speaks again to the central importance of learning, of being able to receive something that is transmitted. In terms of the killing and mutilation in the films, and especially given what we have seen in *Vol.2*, it is markedly benign, more like a charm or spell. It gives the chance of speech and lucidity, a space for the final exchange. The recognition is that for an old-timer the moment of death has come, and is unavoidable. It would not be out of place in many Westerns:

BILL: How do I look?
BEATRIX: You look ready.

This exchange also touches on one other aspect of the couple that is important to this ending, which is the emphasis on absolute youth and age. This has always been a part of the background of the relations between

Pai Mei, Bill and Beatrix: Pai Mei's legendary immense age, Beatrix's marked youth when she is taught by him, Bill's age compared with Beatrix. Which is, of course, a reflection on the two stars, and what we know about them through their films. Part of it is a perception of age: David Carradine (born 1936, first US film a 1964 Western), and Uma Thurman (born 1970, first US film a 1988 college comedy). This is an element in this film but is also much wider; as I have argued elsewhere in this study, Tarantino has produced a body of work that is fascinated by both stars and minor players and what we know about them, part of which is the passing of time for them. This is related to the claim, which is argued at length by Stanley Cavell (1979, pp.74–80), that the players of Hollywood once constituted a world and an anxiety that they now fail to do so.

Happy ending? The lonely world and the luminous star

Before I discuss the meaning of the ending, a preliminary point needs to be made about the *Kill Bill* films, which has to do with these characters' judgements of themselves. At the beginning of *Vol.1*, Beatrix informs us that 'it's mercy, compassion and forgiveness that I lack'. At the beginning of *Vol.2* there is the discussion of the sides in the wedding chapel, and Bill's observation of Beatrix's side, 'Your side was always a bit lonely.' He also tells us, in answer to a plea from Beatrix, that he has never been 'nice' in his whole life. At the very end of *Vol.2*, Beatrix excuses not having told Bill that Pai Mei taught her the exploding heart technique by saying that she is a 'bad person'.

Passing from the couple to the rest of the cast, we might note how much of their relations are casually negative, for reasons that are never explained. Hattori Hanzo makes the deadly sword because of some unknown fact that causes him to wish Bill dead, a feeling that Buddy suggests is one that Bill brings out in people. Elle despises Buddy, and he addresses her as 'you hateful bitch'. Only Buddy, who tells Beatrix he is burying her alive for breaking his brother's heart, feels the need to give a reason for the violent antipathy that is the predominant mode of relation between the adults of the film.

Along with this goes the distance from any positive representations of sexual relations. Bill and Beatrix would be the candidate for this, but significantly we are not shown them together in the past for more than a few moments in the campfire scene that tells the history of Pai Mei. There are, of course, plenty of negative representations: the episodes involving Buck and the trucker initiate the note of sex seen only as a horrific exercise of power, and the point is driven home in *Vol.2* through one memorable image of physical contact between a man and a woman. This is when Beatrix has been shot with the rock salt by Buddy and is again powerless in front of a man. She spits at him: he responds copiously in kind by emptying his mouth in a stream across her vulnerable face. This is what an exchange of body fluids can be reduced to.

Thus *Kill Bill* presents a world of which a dominant characteristic of the relations between many of the adults is violent antipathy. The importance of the children is that they give rise to the only counterweight to this, represented through motherhood (Vernita and Nikki, Beatrix and B.B.) and fatherhood (Bill and B.B.). These minimal families also represent, as I have argued, the state of the ordinary world, or ordinary lives, that in differing ways opens and closes the two films.

In the earlier chapters of this study I have paid attention to Tarantino's interest in endings. I have argued that he favours endings that offer only a limited sight of happiness at best: the ending of the screenplay of *True Romance* in which Clarence dies, the extreme case of the corpses that strew the stage of *Reservoir Dogs*, the final bow in *Pulp Fiction* being taken by the hoods rather than Butch and Fabienne, the recasting of Elmore Leonard's ending in the direction of indicating how little can be made of the good couple in *Jackie Brown*.

What Tarantino seems to be offering in *Vol.2* is a version of the 'happy ending', but one that is aware of the absence of a solid basis for what it might seem to affirm. We see the rescue of a child, the renewed bond between the child and its mother, and the death of the ogre/father, the kidnapper of the little girl. But this image of rescue, these elements of fairy tale, sit in a context in which the parties cannot (can no longer) be identified as the definably good or the evidently bad. The ogre seemed to feed the body and the mind of the little girl as well as anyone, and to be anxious to point out to the mother that she was no better than he.

No account can be given of how B.B. will respond to losing her father – we can only avoid this uncomfortable question by thinking of her as a kind of child of nature, Hawthorne's Pearl or Spenser's Florimell rather than a fully human figure. Beatrix and B.B. seem poised uneasily between an everyday literal world to which they are claiming to have returned and a reading of them as allegorical figures. This is strangely like an American classic that uses the same shattered family group and, after the father dies in another case of unusual heart failure, looks at the mother and child in ways that feel somewhat similar: Hawthorne's *The Scarlet Letter*. Which may go to show that these are not new problems for the American artist.

This is not quite the end of Tarantino's film, which concludes, not with the image of mother and child, but with a long period of concentration, as the extensive credits start to play, on the single face that has dominated both *Vol.1* and *Vol.2*. For perhaps the final way of thinking about these 247 minutes of film is that they represent a remarkable and – in terms of current practice – a very unusual celebration of a single female star. As Tarantino himself has acknowledged, *Kill Bill* could be read as his version of *The Scarlet Empress* (1934), a modern 'relentless excursion into style'. Sternberg's scrupulous description of his film, with its devotion to the presentation of images of Marlene Dietrich – suggestively also cast in a narrative that makes her out to be a kind of monster, the Messalina of the north – seems nicely appropriate. Here as there, a film seems to be given over to opportunities to photograph one face, its masks and its moods: innocent, guilty, shocked, bloodied, soiled, unspotted, in colour, in black and white. This could only be adequately demonstrated by extensive analysis, but to take just one example, look at the images of Beatrix and Elle towards the end of their swordfight, and the strategic, unrealistic contrast between the flawless skin tones of Darryl Hannah's face and the earth still marking Uma Thurman's features. Does Tarantino like combat because of the opportunity it gives to photograph the warrior's face?

Tarantino's insistent reach back into Hollywood's past is marked in a number of details of the presentation of these end credits. He might want to say, this is what the camera could always do, and can still do: to represent the individuality of one human being in such a way as to bring it, and the power of this medium, home to us.

Bibliography

Anderson, Perry (1998) *The Origins of Postmodernity* (London: Verso).

Arendt, Hannah (1968) *The Human Condition* (Chicago: University of Chicago Press).

Baudelaire, Charles (1992) *Selected Writings on Art and Literature* (London: Penguin).

Bernard, Jami (1995) *Quentin Tarantino: the man and his movies* (London: HarperCollins).

Carney, Raymond (1986) *American Vision: the films of Frank Capra* (Cambridge: Cambridge University Press).

Cavell, Stanley (1979) *The World Viewed: reflections on the ontology of film* (enlarged edn) (Cambridge, Mass: Harvard University Press).

Clover, Carol (1992) *Men, Women and Chain Saws: gender in the modern horror film* (London: British Film Institute).

Dawson, Jeff (1995) *Tarantino: inside story* (London: Cassell).

Dyer, Richard (1999) *Seven* (London: British Film Institute).

Fiedler, Leslie A. (1960) *Love and Death in the American Novel* (New York: Criterion).

Fitzgerald, F. Scott (1925/1963) *The Great Gatsby* in *The Bodley Head Scott Fitzgerald: Volume One* (London: Bodley Head).

Frye, Northrop (1957) *Anatomy of Criticism: four essays* (Princeton, NJ: Princeton University Press).

Gallafent, Edward (1994) *Clint Eastwood: actor and director* (London: Studio Vista).

Jackson, Kevin (1990) *Schrader on Schrader* (London: Faber).

James, Henry (1890/1989) *The Tragic Muse* in *Novels 1886–1890* (New York: Library of America).

Knight, Chris (1991) *Blood Relations: menstruation and the origins of culture* (New Haven, Conn.: Yale University Press).

Leonard, Elmore (1981) *City Primeval* (London: W.H. Allen).

Leonard, Elmore (1988) *Touch* (London: Penguin).

Leonard, Elmore (1993) *Rum Punch* (London: Penguin).

Lindberg, Gary (1982) *The Confidence Man in American Literature* (New York: Oxford University Press).

McClung, William Alexander (2000) *Landscapes of Desire: Anglo mythologies of Los Angeles* (Berkeley, Calif.: University of California Press).

Peary, Gerald (ed.) (1998) *Quentin Tarantino: interviews* (Jackson, Miss.: University Press of Mississippi).

Prince, Stephen (ed.) (2000) *Screening Violence* (London: Athlone).

Sartre, Jean-Paul (1955/1968) *Literary and Philosophical Essays* (London: Hutchinson).

Sternberg, Josef von (1965) *Fun in a Chinese Laundry* (New York: Macmillan).

Tarantino, Quentin (1994a) *Pulp Fiction* (London: Faber).

Tarantino, Quentin (1994b) *Reservoir Dogs* (London: Faber).

Tarantino, Quentin (1995a) *Natural Born Killers* (London: Faber).

Tarantino, Quentin (1995b) *True Romance* (London: Faber).

Tarantino, Quentin (1998) *Jackie Brown* (London: Faber).

Truffaut, Francois (1968) *Hitchcock* (London: Secker & Warburg).

Vincendeau, Ginette (2003) *Jean-Pierre Melville: an American in Paris* (London: British Film Institute).

Warner, Marina (1994) *From the Beast to the Blonde: on fairy tales and their tellers* (London: Chatto & Windus).

Warshow, Robert (1962/2001) *The Immediate Experience: movies, comics, theater and other aspects of popular culture* (Cambridge, Mass.: Harvard University Press).

Wood, Robin (1969) *Hitchcock's Films* (London: Zwemmer/New York: A.S. Barnes, second enlarged edition).

Wood, Robin (2002) *Hitchcock's Films Revisited* (New York: Columbia University Press, revised edition).

Further reading

There is too great a mass of writing about Tarantino in both academic and non-academic periodicals, as well as a huge amount of Internet commentary, to consider in this section. I have restricted myself to commenting on some of the books devoted solely to him, and included a couple of cases (Geoff Andrew and Susan Fraiman) in which he is a significant element of a larger project.

Andrew, Geoff (1998) *Stranger than Paradise: maverick film-makers in recent American cinema* (London: Prion).

Geoff Andrew's survey of American independent cinema is a partisan work, making a choice of film-makers whom he feels have 'an individuality and an artistic worth that makes them important' (p.6). With the stated intention of opening up discussion Andrew covers at length David Lynch, John Sayles, Wayne Wang, Jim Jarmusch, the Coen brothers, Spike Lee, Todd Haynes, Steven Soderbergh and Hal Hartley as well as Tarantino. Allowing that Tarantino is a 'cultural phenomenon', Andrew's extended summaries allow him to use detail to describe and analyse the meanings of the plots of the films. The chapter does not shy away from positive judgements: the 'mostly subtle and classical' style of

Reservoir Dogs, and the admiration for the achievement of *Jackie Brown.* The book usefully locates Tarantino in the context of his contemporaries, and is refreshing in its view that value judgements matter.

Barnes, Alan and Marcus Hearn (1996) *Tarantino: A to Zed* (London: Batsford).

Of the popular material produced at the first peak of Tarantino's popularity, this encyclopedia takes itself admirably seriously, treating its subject as 'a fully fledged auteur, not merely as a chancer, stylist, generation hero, passing phenomenon or idiot savant' (p.7). The writers are especially helpful in dealing with contexts and making detailed connections. Entries such as 'heist movies', or the account given of *Man from the South* (the 'Alfred Hitchcock Presents' episode invoked in *Four Rooms*) are exemplary of the book's clarity and usefulness.

Bernard, Jami (1995) *Quentin Tarantino: the man and his movies* (London: HarperCollins).

Bernard's biography, which covers the work up to *Four Rooms,* is based on a wide range of interviews with figures from various periods in Tarantino's career. There are useful accounts of his family background and early life, and interesting detailed commentary on the production histories of the three films that Tarantino wrote with the intention of directing them as his first feature: *True Romance* and *Reservoir Dogs,* and the especially complex case of *Natural Born Killers.* The strategy is to allow the interviewees to speak for themselves rather than attempting to resolve their statements into a tidy narrative.

Botting, Fred and Scott Wilson (2001) *The Tarantinian Ethics* (London: Sage).

Written as part of Nottingham Trent University's Theory, Culture and Society series, Botting and Wilson's book is at a distance from conventional film criticism in that its discussions are based almost entirely on Tarantino's published scripts, rather than the films derived from them. Looking at the scripts in the context of theorists and historians of culture such as Georges Bataille, Jacques Lacan, Emmanuel Levinas and Denis de Rougemont, the authors consider the work under the headings of Personality, Professionalism, Romance, Consumption and Horror. Unsurprisingly, one of the recurrent subjects is Tarantino's use of language, and the book is illuminating on his use of particular terms, such as 'shit' and 'pulp'. The highly sophisticated theoretical understanding of cultural theory can work well, as in the discussion of the charge of racism made against Cliff's 'Sicilian' speech in *True Romance.* Sometimes it seems to overwhelm the context, the dramatic occasion in which specific events happen, such as the extended account of the cultural meanings of tipping, unimpeachable in itself, that introduces the consideration of the moment of conflict over that subject in the opening of *Reservoir Dogs.* The authors look neither back nor forward: the discussions of *True Romance* and *Natural Born Killers* choose to take no note of the films, and that of *Jackie Brown* does not address the adaptation of the Elmore Leonard novel. Towards the end of the book, in the context of Gilles Deleuze's reading of the close-up that is applied mostly to *From Dusk Till Dawn*, some direct address to film as film appears. As one of the most extended critical treatments of Tarantino's output to date, the book poses an important question about the relative status of the word and of the image in contemporary criticism.

Clarkson, Wensley (1995) *Quentin Tarantino: shooting from the hip* (London: Piatkus Books).

Of the 1995 biographies that coincided with the success of *Pulp Fiction*, Clarkson's is the most unashamedly populist. The book takes the form of a dramatisation broken down into acts and scenes, and includes 'end credits' sketching the current activities of the participants, and a list of Tarantino's favourite films. The account of Tarantino's career draws on interviews with many of his collaborators, but even where these are fellow professionals, the bias is towards the personal relations that are entangled with the professional ones. Some of the more interesting moments are the reproduction of documents, such as early readers' vitriolic responses to the screenplay of *True Romance*.

Dawson, Jeff (1995) *Tarantino: inside story* (London: Cassell).

Dawson, the US editor of *Empire* magazine, is somewhat less concerned than Bernard with Tarantino's background and early life, and with his years as a video-store clerk. The accounts of the films incorporate interview material with many of the principal actors, and figures such as the production designers David Wasco and Sandy Reynolds-Wasco. A different set of witnesses of the various pre-production deals surrounding the early films give an account that is usefully complementary to Bernard's.

Fraiman, Susan (2003) *Cool Men and the Second Sex* (New York: Columbia University Press).

Fraiman looks at the way in which gender codes are deployed in the work of a number of writers and film-makers. She begins with Tarantino 'because he offers such a vivid anatomy of "cool" as male rebellion against an "everyday" seated in relationships and implicated in an original dependency' (p.xviii). Although the analyses, largely of *Reservoir Dogs* and *Pulp Fiction*, do address the important subjects of the ordinary, violence, intimacy and the coding of behaviour as masculine or feminine, there is only brief acknowledgement that these are genre narratives working within genre traditions. It would seem that the markedly hostile analyses of the film-makers (Tarantino is followed by Spike Lee) are intended to set up a less minatory account of the scholars who are the subjects of the second half of the study: Edward Said, Andrew Ross and Henry Louis Gates Jr. Fraiman comments that she is 'deeply indebted and strongly allied' (p.xviii) to the scholarship she discusses, but the film-makers seem to be fair game. With its suggestive and important thesis, should this book also be setting up another kind of hierarchy, in which the intellectuals under discussion are 'brilliant' and 'progressive', but the film-makers are turned off into the ambiguous category of the 'charismatic'?

Peary, Gerald (ed.) (1998) *Quentin Tarantino: interviews* (Jackson, Miss.: University Press of Mississippi).

The Tarantino volume of the University of Mississippi's *Conversations with Filmmakers* series reprints 22 interviews with Tarantino and with various collaborators between 1992 and 1997. The material covers press conferences attached to the launch of the films, and some film journalism, of which the most intriguing is perhaps the *Los Angeles Times* piece on Tarantino and Robert Zemekis in conversation. There are also some more academic interviews with *Positif*, *Cahiers du Cinéma* and *Film Comment*; there is some interesting material here on Tarantino's ways of working, both the development of scripts and techniques of directing. Tarantino's reflections on laserdiscs and the very beginning of the DVD market, reprinted from *Entertainment@Home* in 1997, records an interesting point in the history and the economics of home viewing. In all of this, what Harvey Keitel calls Tarantino's 'energy, enthusiasm, intensity, intelligence and vulnerability' (p.37) are in evidence. The book is inevitably a little repetitive but is well edited and indexed.

Polan, Dana (2000) *Pulp Fiction* (London: British Film Institute).

In this volume in the BFI Modern Classics series, Dana Polan investigates contexts of the reception of *Pulp Fiction*, opening with a discussion of websites and turning later to the popular writing on Tarantino. These are interesting areas, although the remit of the book means that it is difficult to see how the specific case of this single film fits into the larger picture of the ways in which the Internet has affected film reception.

Perhaps the most thought-provoking aspect of the book concerns interpretation. In her seminal 1964 polemic 'Against Interpretation', Susan Sontag wrote that 'Interpretation takes the sensory experience of a work of art for granted, and proceeds from there.' Polan concentrates on the sensory experience, and does not desire to proceed from there. He claims that interpretation is beside the point, in part because the film is claimed to be postmodern and 'In post modernism . . . the universe is not to be seen as meaningful' (p.79). More sweepingly, interpretation is presented as defeating the cinematic itself: 'The translation of the whole texture and textuality of an artwork into a verbal message means that tone, feel, the sensuousness of form, and so on, have to be left behind' (p.82), a position that would leave all film criticism out in the cold. It is a pity that the investigation of the 'phenomenon' that is *Pulp Fiction*, the point with which Polan begins and ends, is offered as complementary to a hostility to interpretation, and I would question whether the use of 'postmodernism' as a default description of current American culture is a really helpful one here.

Index

Index

Pulp Fiction, 2, 3, 4, 19, 21–9, 40, 45–51, 54, 66, 67, 71–80, 84, 100, 119

Raging Bull, 86
Red River, 24
Reservoir Dogs, 2, 3, 4, 6, 8, 12–20, 21, 28, 32, 40–5, 50, 61, 67–71, 72, 84, 100, 101, 102, 119
Reynolds-Wasco, Sandy, 70
Rififi, 9, 12
Rio Bravo, 13
Rum Punch, 4, 85, 87–90, 97

Sartre, Jean-Paul, 4, 84
Satie, Erik, 60
Scarlet Empress, The, 99, 120
Scarlet Letter, The, 119
Schlesinger, John, 85
Schrader, Paul, 3, 85, 86, 88, 90–4, 96–7
Schwarzenegger, Arnold, 45
Scorsese, Martin, 86
Scott, Tony, 55, 95
seriousness, 5–6
Seven, 39
sexual abuse, 56, 64, 104
Shogun Assassin, 117
silence, 61–2, 63, 65
Sinatra, Nancy, 101
slavery, 22, 25, 28
Sobchack, Vivian, 39
Spenser, Edmund, 119
Sternberg, Josef von, 99
Stone, Oliver, 59, 63–5

Taxi Driver, 86
technologies, 73, 84
Touch, 3 , 85, 87–94, 96–7
Tourneur, Jacques, 54
tradition, 2, 7, 19–20, 27, 51, 73, 78, 98
True Romance, 2, 4, 52–9, 60, 61, 63, 84, 95
Twain, Mark, 17, 19, 60

Unforgiven, 20
uniform, 13
Unmarried Woman, An, 97

Van Doren, Mamie, 74
Vian, Boris, 84
Vincendeau, Ginette, 5
violence, 4, 13, 16–17, 38–51, 55–6, 61–2, 102, 112

Warner, Marina, 50
Warshow, Robert, 5, 21
Weir, Peter, 86
westerns, 14, 20, 51, 83, 86–7, 92, 96–7, 112, 117
West, Nathanael, 85
widescreen, 72
Wild Bunch, The, 5, 11, 116
Wilder, Billy, 7
Wilson, Scott, 123
Wizard of Oz, The, 100–1
Womack, Bobby, 84
Wood, Robin, 5, 13
Working Girl, 53